# BUILDING COMMUNITY

# BUILDING COMMUNITY

**THE WORK OF ESKEW+DUMEZ+RIPPLE**

# CONTENTS

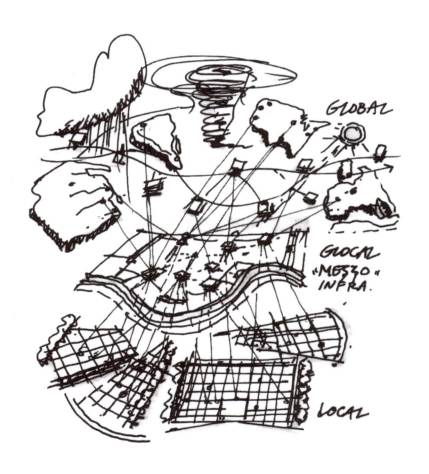

## DESIGN MÉLANGE

"often a concoction of incongruous elements"
BILL MORRISH

Building community is the same worldwide — it is a universal instinct. But building a city's *civic capacity*, its ability to bring together divergent interests and operate within complex ecological situations, is different. As architects, Eskew+Dumez+Ripple leverage this circumstance into productive traction from which they shape and construct buildings, urban landscapes and social communities. Their work is emotionally rooted in a New Orleans/ Gulf Coast design tradition — what the architectural historian Dell Upton describes as the process of seeing that buildings, gardens and cities are more than historic form types, but a physical manifestation of an evolving cultural ecology.

The Louisiana geographer and anthropologist Fred B. Kniffen called this regional cultural ecology a *mélange*. His fieldwork on Louisiana and Gulf Coast vernacular architecture reveals that these modest buildings and landscape are sophisticated designs, a brilliant concoction of responses to the region's varied environments, a synthesis of different ethnic and global cultures, expressed with a richness of ingredients that is formed into an elegant, multilayered set of interior and exterior spaces and enlivened by a hybrid aesthetic patois.

I have used these vernacular terms intentionally to communicate how this firm combines history, community and modernity in their work. Pursuing a course of architectural creation based on design mélange means that they work in the everyday blend of private, political, social and ecological life to reveal the places and lines of incongruity that exist in all community building

processes. Ecologists know these places of divergent habitat as robust eco-tones. As civic leaders, Eskew+Dumez+Ripple know that these lines of conflict can be, once identified, confidently transformed. A design mélange is a hybrid resolution that brings together these points of conflict, differing interests and dynamic ecologies into a vibrant and nurturing environment through a social and cultural dialogue of architectural creation. *Mélange* requires an attitude where education and social design settings are central. It is a generative form of architectural process that produces not just buildings; rather, it is a civic act of setting the terms of social equity, community connection and hope in the city and its future. The designs are developed through an extensive set of interpersonal exchanges and hands-on design transactions that operate in small neighborhood meetings on front porches, in the local seafood restaurants, in builders' workshops, artists' studios, church meeting halls or the hallways of City Hall. The act of design mélange requires that the architects literally draw out the participants to become active architectural agents and champions. By turning clients and residents into active agents, the studio brings forth a wealth of ideas and ingredients that elevate the built work into a fine gumbo of delicate seasonings and distinct elements enlivened with a patois of elegant details. The process reveals ecological micro-climates and delineates cultural moments that add a unique accent or dialectic to each project.

# INTRODUCTION
REED KROLOFF

How many New Orleanians does it take to change a light bulb? Three: one to change the bulb, and two to reminisce about how great the old bulb used to be.

This anecdote neatly summarizes the challenge faced by Eskew+Dumez+Ripple (EDR), the modernist architectural practice based in New Orleans. Music, food and literature all go down smoothly in the Big Easy. Change doesn't. Especially not change that offers any challenge to the city's highly refined sense of itself, one that as far as architecture is concerned, closed the book some time before Edward VII ascended to the throne of England. The result is a place that within its historic core is romantic, small-scale and surprisingly consistent. There is modern architecture in the city, to be sure, but it is the exception, not the rule.

Is the term "New Orleans modern," then, an oxymoron, or worse yet, an impossibility? Happily, no. There is a Modernist heritage in New Orleans. And though, understandably, it starts later than in many American cities, it comes on with a bang: in 1955, the second year of the vaunted Progressive Architecture (now P/A) awards, 5 of the 35 prizes awarded went to New Orleans architects doing work in their own city—more than any other city, state or region that year. Architects like Albert Ledner, Charles Colbert, John Lawrence, and Nathaniel Curtis and Arthur Davis captured the attention of the national architectural press with designs that were starkly different from the trellis-and-scrollwork standard of the French Quarter and Garden District. Curtis

and Davis, who would go on to design the American Hospital in Berlin; the Department of Health, Education and Welfare in Washington, DC; and perhaps most famously, the Louisiana Superdome, blazed the brightest trail. The consistent high quality of their work and the firm's ability to land projects both at home and abroad (here adopting the New Orleanian understanding of abroad, which means out of town), demonstrated that if all the stars were in alignment, if the dice were stuck on sevens, and if lightning actually did strike twice, a modernist practice could in fact be built in the city.

Eskew+Dumez+Ripple now occupies the position once held by Curtis and Davis. It is the most respected architectural practice in New Orleans, an office with more awards than they can count politely (including, yes, one or two from P/A), and commissions from Montana to Florida. Its principals are popular lecturers and jurors across the country; two are AIA Fellows. Their clients include institutions, developers, and state and local governments, and their portfolio ranges from museums and cultural buildings to planning, healthcare and education. The practice maintains a staff of 40 people in a dramatic studio perched atop one of the city's tallest buildings, with a miles-long view of the Mississippi River and all of the French Quarter and Uptown. Things are good there.

How? How is it they can thrive in an environment that seems so poorly suited to this kind of endeavor? Not only is New Orleans not naturally predisposed to appreciate modern architecture, the city has been in a state of near-perpetual economic decline since, well, since some time after the Civil War. There have been periods of growth and excitement, to be sure. But during the years in which EDR has been plying its trade, New Orleans has not been at the leading edge of either economic or architectural trends.

Yet the firm has flourished. This is partly due to a good, simple management structure and inspired leadership from the firm's principals. But it is also due to a wonderful inversion of the design formula that brought success to Lawrence, Colbert, and Curtis and Davis in 1955. Those architects embraced the fundamental abstraction of modernism as a point of departure and then inflected it quietly toward the context of New Orleans. EDR, by contrast, revels in the complicated reality of New Orleans and then abstracts it to create a modern architecture that transcends its very particular place, an architecture that may be born of Louisiana but is not necessarily beholden to it.

Consider two projects. First is the Louisiana State Museum in Baton Rouge, completed in 2005, and the recipient of peer-reviewed design awards at the city, state, regional and national levels. Above all, it is a beautiful building: a solid yet restrained volume anchoring a corner of the Louisiana State Capitol complex. Wrapped in a tight skin of metal and glass and set atop a white concrete base, the museum is a respectful companion to the Depression-Deco extravagance of Huey Long's state capitol tower, and a crisp, silvery contrast to the surrounding canopy of live oak trees. On three sides, the museum is a buttoned-up essay in minimalism, the kind of refined architectural statement one might expect to house an important art collection or symphony hall. It fairly radiates high culture. But round the building facing west, and a different story awaits. There, a gigantic opening in the façade reveals a courtyard carved deep into the building. It is a cool, covered space with a long reflecting pool. Light filters through a series of slots above and to the side, creating an architectural analog to the diaphanous atmosphere beneath the trees beyond and a welcome respite to the watery heat of a Louisiana afternoon. The volume of the space, which reaches the full height and nearly half the depth of the building, fractures the otherwise solid composition and creates a chamber scaled to respond to the 450-foot height of the capitol without challenging the older building's supremacy.

It also carves out an impressive forecourt for the museum, a sort of internalized, gigantic front porch. Front porches are one of the primary features of New Orleans architecture, the hallmark of the city's picturesque Victorian "shotgun" houses. With a shotgun, the porch is an appendage, an additive element. At the State Museum, by contrast, it is a subtraction, the opening of a space within the volume of the building. Volumetric subtraction is, of course, a modernist trope. Further, what is a porch? It is a transitional element, a place between inside and out, an architectural pause. With the subtraction, EDR inverts and thus abstracts the form. But the precedent is honored, nonetheless: Their porch still suspends the journey from outside to in; it is still a place to stop and gather before entering the building. In other words, with the State Museum, EDR celebrates local conditions but transcends local convention. Their take on tradition engages the spatial and processional qualities of Louisiana architecture, not its decorative embellishments.

The same is true of the recently completed residential tower at 930 Poydras in downtown New Orleans, though the translation is less conspicuous. Here, the architects hoist an essential typology—the French Quarter courtyard townhouse—into the air in an attempt to enrich the typically limited environment of high-rise rental real estate. The building itself is a standard program: a 21 story, L-shaped tower of 250 apartments stacked on top of a solid 8-floor block of parking. The site, on the busy main street of the city's financial core, is unremarkable, though it does offer panoramic views of the downtown area.

Those views are accessed through an innovative skin of syncopated glass and metal panels that alternate as the building rises to make it increasingly transparent with each ascending floor. This has the triple effect of screening the lower-level parking, opening the upper residential floors to light and views and creating a variegated surface pattern that is unique on each side of the structure yet somehow visually consistent overall. The windows are also very tall and thin, due to the fact that each spans two floors behind it. In any other city, that might just be a neat trick. In New Orleans, it is a clear reference to the proportions of traditional glazing in the French Quarter (and

later, the Uptown neighborhoods, as well), which took its shape originally in response to the high-ceilinged interiors of French Quarter buildings designed to encourage the city's warm, moist air to rise up and out. The reference here is purely visual, as 930 Poydras is air-conditioned.

The more complicated precedent reference to the Quarter rests in a sky lobby and terrace located on the ninth floor. The glazed lobby hangs out over Poydras, a reminder of French Quarter arcades, and like those balcony spaces, a gesture to the street below that life goes on at the upper levels, as well. The terrace is a play on the Quarter's famed hidden courtyards, the secret inner world of that city within a city, and the inspiration for writers, poets and musicians for hundreds of years. At 930 Poydras, the courtyard isn't hidden behind a street-level door, but behind what is the true "door" of high-rise living, the elevator. Guests and residents entering from the ground or garage must stop and transfer on the ninthth floor, where, as they pass through the door of the elevator lobby—as one might pass through a passageway in the Quarter, they encounter the surprise of a (sky-) courtyard, a generous public gathering space for residents and guests. And like so many courtyards in the Quarter, it is landscaped, has a water feature (in this case, a pool) and windows that look out on it from other residential spaces. It is at once a retreat and a lively public space.

It could be argued that this comparison requires a modest leap of faith, but at some level, so does everything in New Orleans.

And without a doubt, the architect's intent is sincere. Too many of the firm's projects — no matter where they are located — reflect the same level of consideration, even when they move to more primal issues. I have always been particularly intrigued with a small, unbuilt proposal for a swimming pool, which, like the work of their 1955 predecessors, won EDR a P/A design award (in 2000). It is a modest enclosure, barely bigger than a bedroom, but it is dense with allusion and inventive craft. Above is a sunbathing deck adjacent to a rectangular latex membrane. Below is a small pool, enclosed by a grid of wood slats and the latex above. As the latex fills with water (from the daily summer showers in New Orleans), it sags into the space below, oozing water and milky yellow light. The air is moist and warm and thick, and the water drips slowly through the latex and into the pool. This is a mysterious, womblike place, strange yet comforting.

Before architecture, before the city, New Orleans was a swamp, a vast, murky underworld of towering trees, still water and the funk of decay and creation. The pool room, with its pure, cubic form and its pendulous, watery cover is an allegory for the collision of architecture and nature in a place like New Orleans. The architecture is crisp and formal, but nature — irregular, unpredictable and foreboding — is not. What rests between — the close, uneasy balance — is life in that city, and more generally, life on this planet.

New Orleans is an old city, one of fundamentals. Despite its battering over the years by nature and by humans, it remains a repository for messages of faith, resilience, renewal, craft, tradition and invention. These are lodged in its food, its music, and yes, its architecture. Eskew+Dumez+Ripple interprets the messages it finds in that architecture with uncommon grace and wisdom. This volume is ample evidence that the truths the firm uncovers resonate far beyond their geographic origin.

## LOUISIANA STATE MUSEUM
BATON ROUGE, LOUISIANA

This state history museum is located adjacent to the Louisiana State Capitol and Gardens within the governmental complex now known as Capitol Park. The project is the sole cultural institution included in an ambitious master planning effort to relocate 1.5 million square feet of dispersed state governmental offices into a consolidated location surrounding the historic Capitol Tower, built in 1932 by then governor Huey Long.

A previously adopted master plan for Capitol Park dictated that all new structures built on the Capitol grounds were to be designed to reference the Art Deco character of the existing Capitol Tower. An alternate strategy for the State Museum was proposed, suggesting that a distinction be made between new governmental office buildings and proposed cultural facilities within the campus. This strategy allowed for a design that provides a powerful relationship between landscape and architecture in order to acknowledge the unique conditions of its program and site.

The new museum is located across Fourth Street from the State Library, built in 1958. Fourth Street is both the primary and symbolic entrance onto the Capitol Grounds, connecting the Capitol to the City of Baton Rouge. The museum siting establishes biaxial symmetry with the State Library to the west while acknowledging its privileged location adjacent to the Gardens and Tower to the north. The museum can be approached from either of these directions, and visitors converge at a large, covered terrace — an overscaled "porch" — that opens to the north to provide framed views of the Capitol Tower. Entry to the museum is from this terrace, and a multipurpose room (designed to accommodate 200 seats for lectures or 100 for banquets) opens directly onto this outdoor gathering space for expanded events.

The envelope of the building is composed of cast-in-place concrete, glass, and metal wall panels. The fenestration and façade compositions of the museum were designed to respond to the varying context, bridging between the monumentality of the civic buildings to the west, north and south and the smaller, residential scale of the single-family bungalows to the east. On the west façade, the metal wall panels transition from solid to perforated at the entry terrace, where the simple cubic volume gestures toward the Capitol Tower. This perforated screen wall acts as a scrim to filter daylight into the space and changes in character from a shimmering, silvery object by day to a translucent, glowing presence at night.

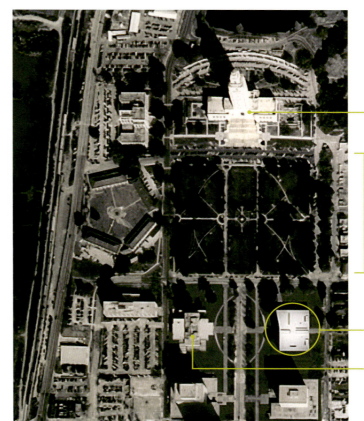

Capitol Tower

Capitol Gardens

State Museum

State Library

The museum occupies the former site of a 3.25-acre surface parking lot. The building's siting was configured to preserve all eight of the existing century-old live oak trees and two large mature magnolias. The project transformed almost 2 acres of asphalt paving into landscaped green, significantly reducing storm-water runoff.

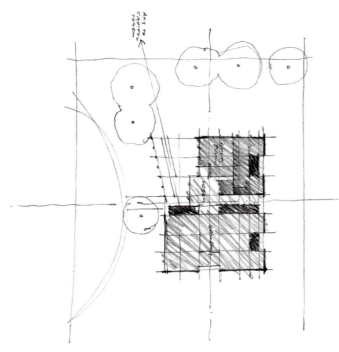

Site Sketch

Daylighting / Solar Control Diagram

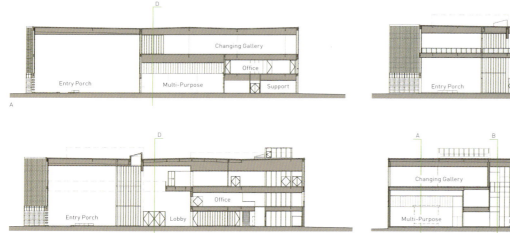

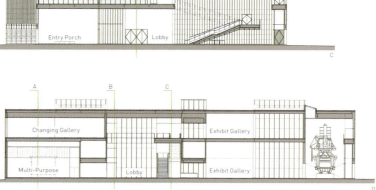

Changing Gallery

Office

Entry Porch
Multi-Purpose
Support

A

Entry Porch
Lobby

C

Entry Porch

Office

Lobby

B

Changing Gallery
Exhibit Gallery

Multi-Purpose
Lobby
Exhibit Gallery

D

Building Sections

The program includes both permanent exhibition and changing exhibit galleries. Technical specifications for permanent exhibition galleries required a 24-foot-high clear space. This volumetric prerequisite allowed administrative offices to be located within a second-floor "mezzanine," maximizing program uses within the available building envelope and reducing the building footprint.

The glass and metal hanging sculpture, titled "River of Memory", by Alexander Tylevich, was installed in the museum's double volume lobby as a result of the State of Louisiana's Percent for Art Program.

Third-Floor Plan

Second-Floor Plan

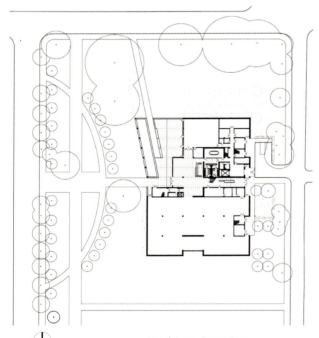

Site / First-Floor Plan

| | |
|---|---|
| Client | State of Louisiana, Department of Culture, |
| | Recreation & Tourism |
| Architect of Record | Eskew+Dumez+Ripple |
| Project Team | R. Allen Eskew, Steve Dumez, Tracy Lea, Vincent Bandy, |
| | Jose Alvarez, Robert Kleinpeter, Sebastian Salvado, |
| | Byron Mouton, Rick Dupont, Kevin Morris, |
| | Shannon Downey Tufts,  Matt Kymes |
| General Contractor | Carothers Construction, Inc. |
| Landscape Architect | Jon Emerson and Associates |
| Structural & Civil Engineer | McKee & Deville Consulting Engineers, Inc. |
| MEP Engineer | M & E Consultants |
| Exhibit Designer | Christopher Chadbourne & Associates |
| Exhibit Consultant | ExPlus Inc. |
| Museum Programmer | M. Goodwin & Associates, Inc. |
| Lighting Designer | PHA Lighting Design |
| Cost Estimator | Oppenheim Lewis, Inc. |
| Photographer | Timothy Hursley |

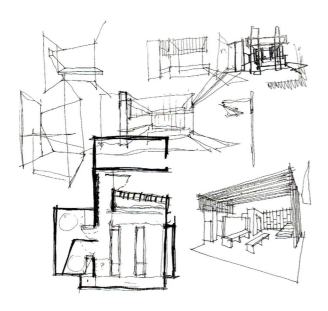

# KATE AND LAURANCE EUSTIS CHAPEL
NEW ORLEANS, LOUISIANA

This small interdenominational chapel within an existing hospital was commissioned by a large medical institution to more effectively serve the spiritual needs of the hospital's patients, families and staff. As an interdenominational facility, the chapel could not rely on specific religious symbols or iconography in order to assert its claim as sacred space. Instead, the design proposal introduces more universal themes of healing and reconciliation to engage visitors with the spiritual.

Seen from the main hospital corridor, the new chapel manifests a mysterious, luminous presence. A high window provides a partial view to an enigmatic wood scrim. Light emanates from within the chapel through a stained-glass wall narrowing to a vestibule recessed off the hospital corridor. On the opposite wall, a list of donor names glow in backlit relief, appropriately shining additional light on the entry to the chapel.

Inside the chapel, three distinct spaces were created to satisfy the project program — a main worship space (seating a maximum of 12) along with two smaller rooms for counseling or private meditation. Immediately upon entering the main space, one is transported out of the institutional hospital environment and into a realm of the senses. The calming sound of water is immediately apparent, and the dramatic change in lighting begins to presage entry to a more serene, contemplative space.

As one enters the volume of the worship space, one becomes aware of a woven wood ceiling that envelopes and defines the seating area. Seemingly untethered and floating within the room, this wooden "shroud" hovers over visitors like a luminescent curtain. Daylight spills in from a concealed window near the fountain source, whose water washes along the interior surface of the rough plaster wall before dropping into a basin beneath a set of cast-glass tablets. This cast-glass shelf, lit from below, glows within the chapel as a repository for personal artifacts or mementos visitors may bring to the space while praying.

In contrast to traditional religious space, this small chapel deals less with celebratory gathering and more with personal meditation and individual reflection. As one confronts issues of personal joy or sorrow, it provokes a kind of indelible wonder while still affording the traditional sanctuary of religious architecture — a place of peace apart from the frenzy of contemporary life.

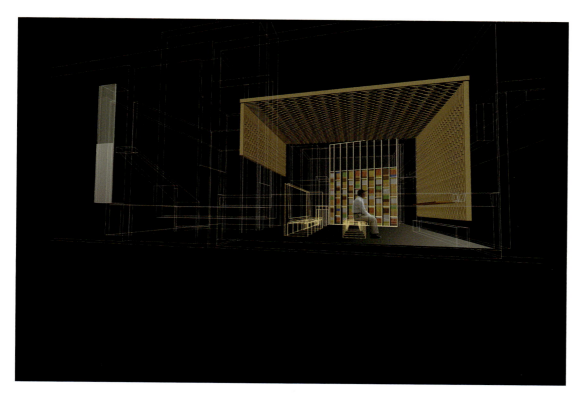

Occupying the area created by the relocation of the previous hospital entry due to a major critical care expansion, the new chapel affords greater visibility to patients and families, as well as access to natural light.

In addition to the primary gathering space, two adjacent rooms were designed for more intimate meditation and prayer. Each is given a window to bring in natural light and provide focus for reflection.

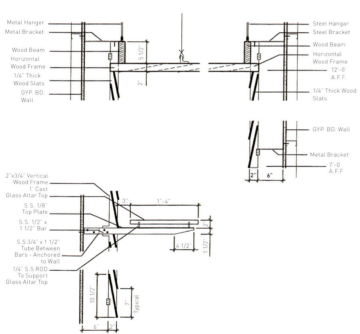

Metal Hanger
Metal Bracket

Wood Beam
Horizontal
Wood Frame
1/4" Thick
Wood Slats
GYP. BD.
Wall

5 1/2"

2"

Steel Hangar
Steel Bracket

Wood Beam
Horizontal
Wood Frame
12'-0"
A.F.F.

1/4" Thick Wood
Slats

GYP. BD. Wall

Metal Bracket

7'-0
A.F.F

2"    6"

2"x3/4" Vertical
Wood Frame
1' Cast
Glass Altar Top

S.S. 1/8"
Top Plate

S.S. 1/2" x
1 1/2" Bar

S.S 3/4" x 1 1/2"
Tube Between
Bars - Anchored
to Wall

1/4" S.S ROD
To Support
Glass Altar Top

3"       1"-4"

2"

4 1/2"    1 1/2"

10 1/2"    7"
Typical

6"    2"

Section Detail through Wood Shroud

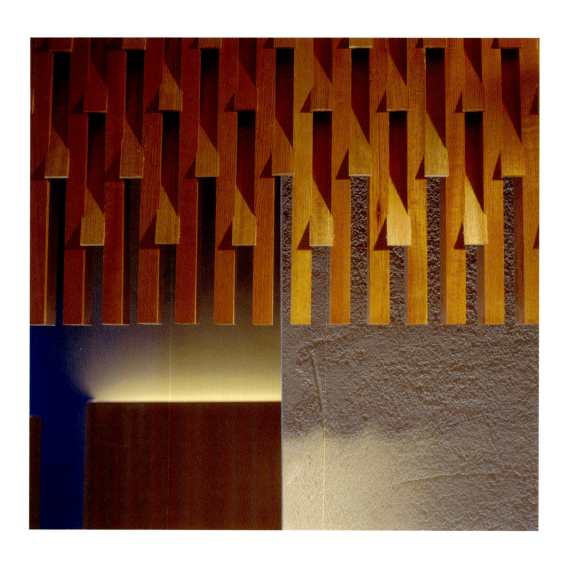

| | |
|---|---|
| Client | Ochsner Clinic Foundation |
| Architect of Record | Eskew+Dumez+Ripple |
| Project Team | Steve Dumez, Charles Hite, Byron Mouton, |
| | Shannon Downey Tufts, Sebastian Salvado, |
| | Robert Kleinpeter |
| MEP Engineer | Smith Seckman Reid, Inc. |
| General Contractor | Construction South |
| Art Glass Fabrication | Dependable Glass |
| Millwork Fabrication | Axis Construction |
| Photographers | Timothy Hursley |
| | Neil Alexander (pg. 32, 37-40) |

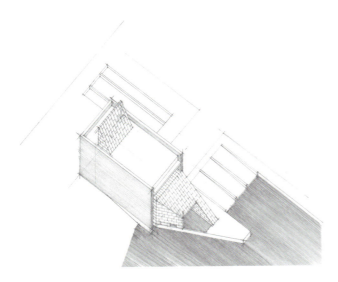

## ESTUARINE HABITATS & COASTAL FISHERIES CENTER

LAFAYETTE, LOUISIANA

The Estuarine Habitat & Coastal Fisheries Center was designed as part of a joint federal/university research campus in Lafayette, Louisiana dedicated to the study of coastal marine life and their habitats. The physical program for this facility includes wet and dry laboratories, conference center, and administrative and research offices for the National Marine Fisheries Service, the U.S. Fish & Wildlife Service, the U.S. Army Corps of Engineers and the Smithsonian Institution.

The social program, however, is one of making connections: connections internally between the Center's various federal divisions and externally with both the public and the adjacent university campus. To that end, two critical spaces were added during the design phase: an Interpretive Gallery, which serves to present the mission of the Center to the visiting public, and a two-story "commons," which promotes interaction among the Center's various users and acts as the social heart of the facility.

The program is organized into two distinct wings, derived from a careful analysis of user needs and cost/energy efficiencies related to the mix of office and laboratory system requirements. From the standpoint of security, the offices act as a buffer between the public functions of the building (Conference Center and Interpretive Gallery) and the more private and secure areas of the laboratories.

The arrangement of the program is visually expressed in the architectural treatment of the various spaces on the exterior. Offices are clad in metal panels, while the more fixed public and laboratory spaces are solidly clad in brick masonry. The southwest elevation overlooks a manmade wetlands habitat that signals to the public the research aims of the facility. Here, the metal face of the office wing includes a brise-soleil to protect windows from the harsh afternoon sun while also reflecting daylight deep into the offices for energy efficiency. The Interpretive Gallery is the most expressive element of the design, announcing itself as the primary public space of the facility. Here, a "light box" clad in lead-coated copper shingles extends outward to capture a small reflecting pool, which projects the play of light on water into the room and connects the space to the larger habitat just outside.

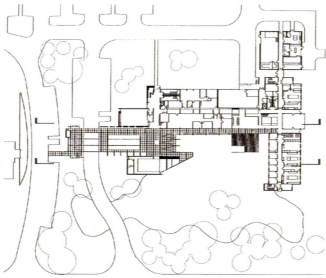

First Floor Plan

The wetlands habitat, a signature feature of the facility, operates at levels both functional and symbolic. Functionally, the habitat supports the wastewater discharge needs of the facility. Symbolically, the habitat reinforces the visual, physical and research linkage with the adjacent National Wetlands Research Center by extending the wetlands across the face of both facilities.

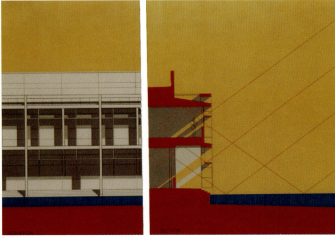

Elevation                    Section

The Interpretive Gallery is designed to provide for a variety of functions that include gallery style displays, lectures and public presentations as a part of the educational outreach efforts of the federal agencies.

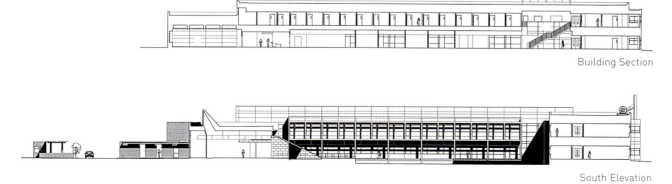

Building Section

South Elevation

Stairs connecting after first and second floors are provided with expansive areas of glazing and lined with warm wood treatments for natural light and views.

| | |
|---|---|
| Client | U.S. Department of Commerce |
| Architect of Record | Eskew+Dumez+Ripple / Guidry Beazley, A Joint Venture |
| Project Team | R. Allen Eskew, Steve Dumez, Charles Hite, B.J. Siegel, |
| | Peter Doncaster, Greg Gardiol, Debra Warner, Jennifer Calla, |
| | Nick Marshall, Gabriel Smith |
| General Contractor | Woodrow Wilson Construction Company |
| Landscape Architect | Jon Emerson & Associates |
| Structural Engineer | McKee and Deville Consulting Engineers, Inc. |
| MEP Engineer | Associated Design Group, Inc. |
| Civil Engineer | Pensco, Inc. |
| Environmental Engineer | W.S. Neef & Associates |
| Lighting Design | Cline Bettridge Bernstein Lighting Design, Inc. |
| Geotechnical Engineer | Woodward-Clyde |
| Laboratory Design | Earl Walls Associates |
| Photographer | Timothy Hursley |

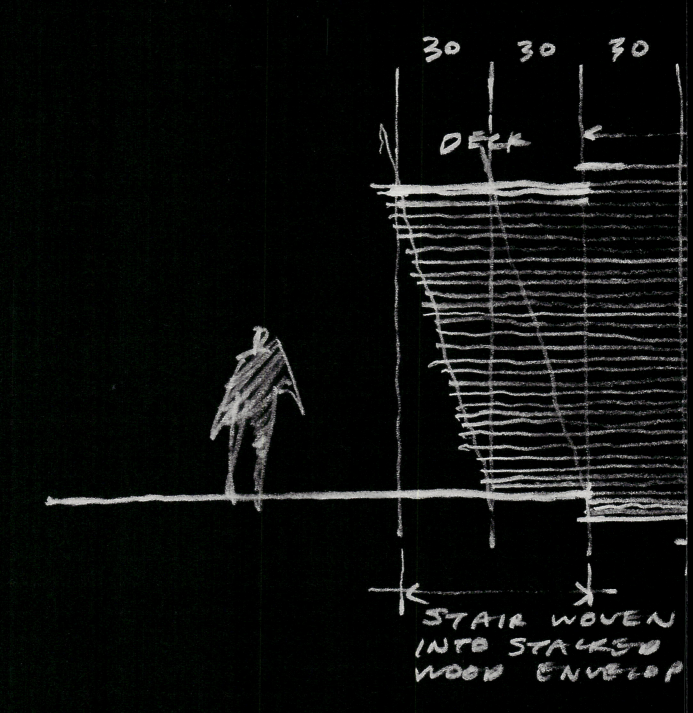

30        30        30

DECK

STAIR WOVEN
INTO STAKED
WOOD ENVELOP

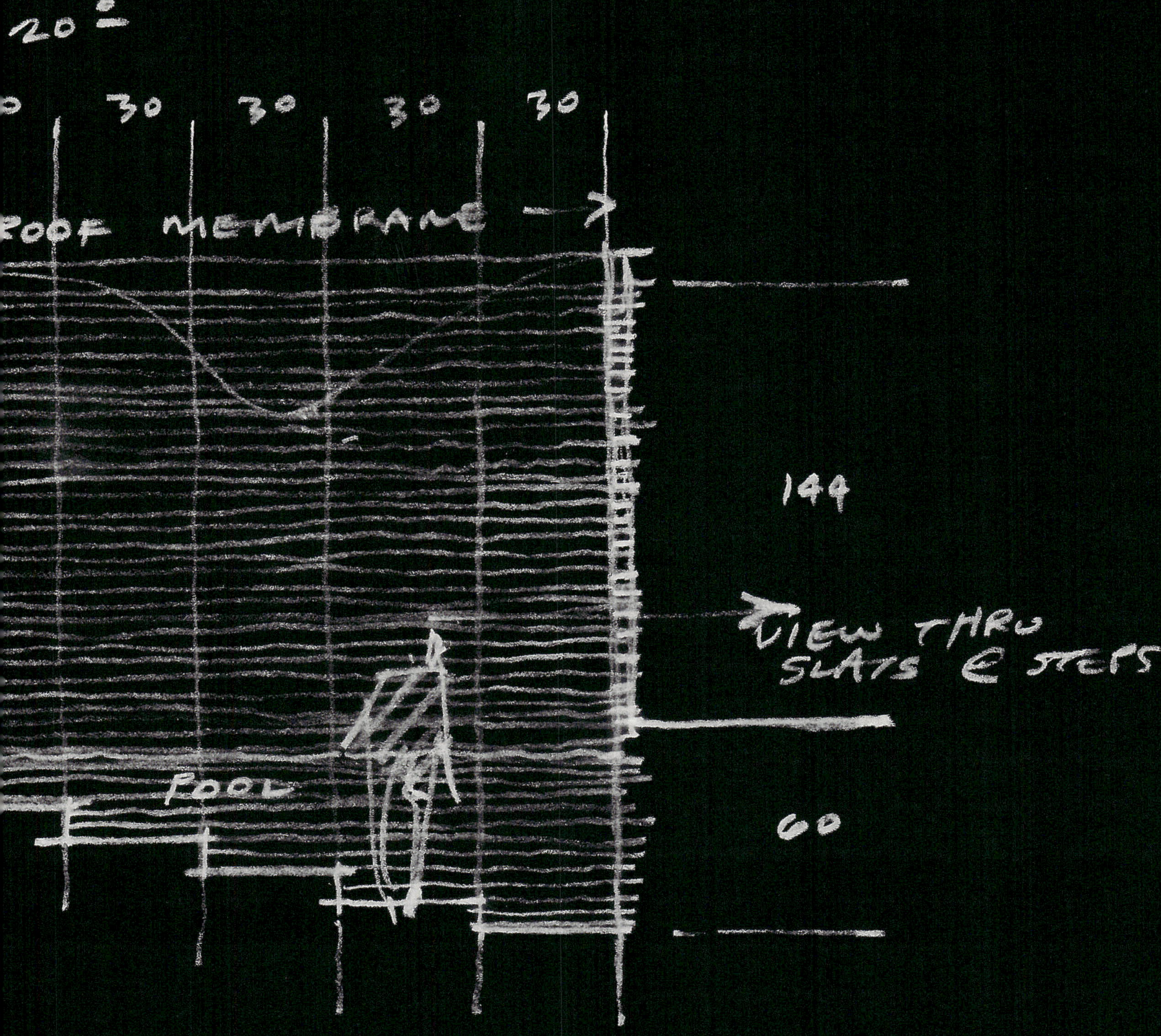

20²

0   30      30      30      30

ROOF   MEMBRANE →

144

VIEW THRU
SLATS @ STEPS

POOL

60

## WHITE LINEN BATHING PAVILION

NEW ORLEANS, LOUISIANA

Enjoyed alone or shared with others, this small pavilion is intended for relaxation or reflection amongst cool water, musty earth and warm sunlight. At once corporeal and spiritual, the project encourages the body and mind in pleasure and daydreaming, healing and contemplation, conversation and thought.

A shallow pool is constructed of poured-in-place concrete, where the scent and feel of the earth is immediate and direct. The pool affords a cool spot where one can escape the heat of the day and relax in the privacy of dappled shade. Its connection to grottoes and classical baths is intentional and, as such, resonates with its intended use as a place for intimate gathering or private meditation.

The enclosure is a quill-like weave of cypress that permits light and air to flow through the pavilion with no loss of privacy. Its stacked construction echoes the practical directness of wood boards in the lumber yard or freight pallets at the quayside. From its exterior, the pavilion assumes a spirit of mystery and enigma; from the interior, one of privacy and enclosure.

The roof leaks. A specialized elastic fabric is used as both a collector for water and a ceiling above the in-ground pool. Primarily used for sunbathing, the fabric periodically fills with rainwater and distends into the space below. As the water accumulates, the specialized weave of the fabric is designed to fail and the sac will begin to weep, dripping water into the pool below and connecting the two bodies in an intricate dance of water.

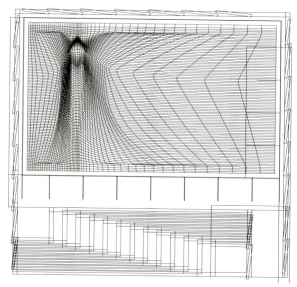

Roof Plan

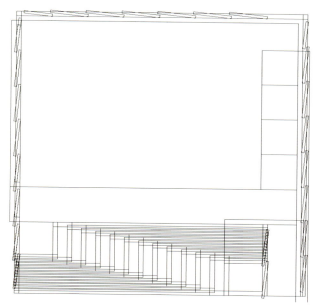

Floor Plan

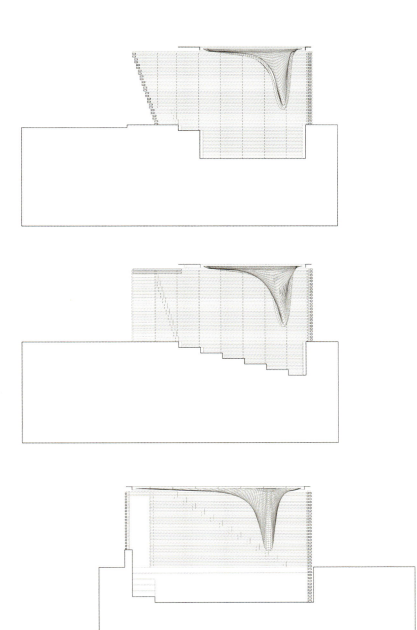

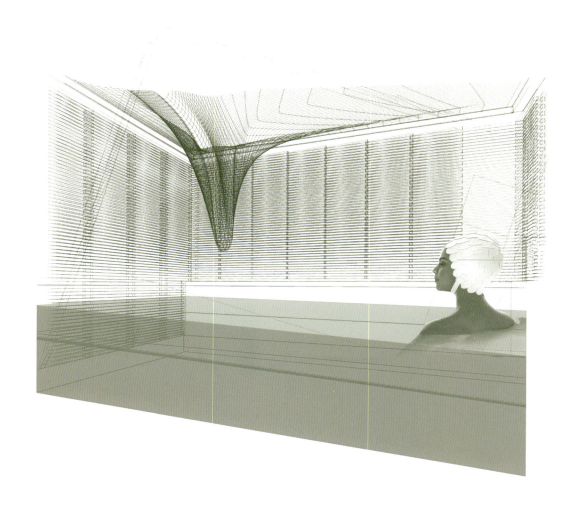

| | |
|---|---|
| Architect of Record | Eskew+Dumez+Ripple |
| Project Team | Steve Dumez, R. Allen Eskew, B.J. Siegel, Matthew Kymes, Nick Marshall, Jose Alvarez, Marianne Makdisi |
| Membrane Consultant | Ove Arup & Partners |
| Photographer | Neil Alexander |

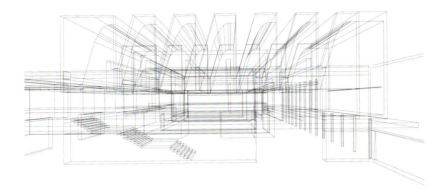

## ACADIANA CENTER FOR THE ARTS

LAFAYETTE, LOUISIANA

The Acadiana Center for the Arts serves to support the varied activities of the Lafayette artistic community in one dynamic and interactive location, providing a multifaceted venue for performing and visual arts presentations and education.

The first phase of this multiphase project involved the complete renovation of an existing vacant bank building in downtown Lafayette. The original masonry and stone exterior shell and cast-in-place concrete structure were repurposed to provide a variety of art exhibition spaces along with education classrooms and offices for the Arts Council of Acadiana.

The primary exhibition space, a 5,000-square-foot Changing Exhibit Gallery, was created within the double-height volume of the former bank lobby.  During its prior life as a banking hall, large vertical windows beginning 8 feet above the floor provided daylight to the space while maintaining privacy from the street. In converting the space for gallery use, we introduced a continuous,

translucent band of sliding glass panels that allow filtered natural light into the gallery while providing an uninterrupted wall for art display. This glazing treatment continues on the opposite (inside) wall of the gallery, providing a visual connection to the second floor "art house" spaces where a bay window projects into the gallery volume. Support spaces and Arts Council offices are organized around a plywood-clad, multistory volume containing a smaller Changing Exhibits Gallery at the first floor and a multipurpose education classroom at the second.

Phase II, currently under construction, will provide a new public lobby/café for the center, along with a 300-seat multipurpose studio theater. The theater is designed to support a variety of musical and theatrical performances with configurations that vary from an open room with up to 6,000 square feet of flat floor space to multiple theater seating arrangements that include proscenium, thrust, black box or theater in the round.

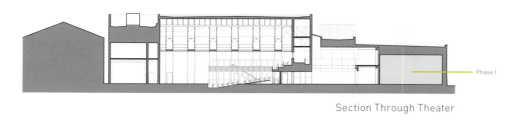

Section Through Theater

Section Through Lobby

Phase I

Phase I

These sections depict the Phase II expansion performing arts theater. The venue is designed to seat 300 in an intimate setting with telescoping first-level seats that run below grade to accommodate a variety of seating configurations.

Artist's rendering of future Phase II street façade.

The Changing Exhibits Gallery provides 5,000 square feet
of space for flexible displays of art. Gallery installation of
paintings by Willie Birch.

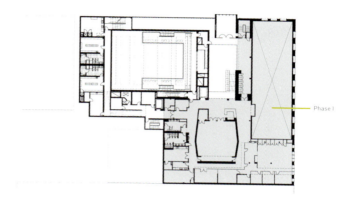

Phase I

Second Floor Plan

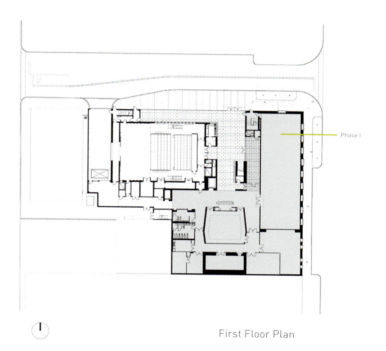

Phase I

First Floor Plan

| | |
|---|---|
| Client | Lafayette Consolidated Government |
| Architect of Record | Eskew+Dumez+Ripple (Prime, Phase I), |
| | Architects Southwest (Phase II) |
| Design Architect | Eskew+Dumez+Ripple (Phase II) |
| Project Team | R. Allen Eskew, Steve Dumez, Kurt Hagstette, Vicki Smith, |
| | Nick Marshall, Robert Kleinpeter, Sebastian Salvado, |
| | Gabriel Smith, Kevin Morris, Blaise Durio, Kimberly Tseng |
| General Contractor | Belltech Group (Phase I), The Lemoine Company (Phase II) |
| Structural Engineer | McKee and Deville Consulting Engineers, Inc. |
| MEP Engine | M & E Consultants |
| Civil Engineer | McKee and Deville Consulting Engineers, Inc. |
| Museum Planner | M. Goodwin Associates, Inc. (Phase I) |
| Theater Programmer | Robert Long & Associates (Phase II) |
| Theater Design | Theatre Projects Consultants (Phase II) |
| Acoustic Consultant | Akoustiks Consultants (Phase II) |
| Photographer | Chipper Hatter |

# THE ARCHITECT AS ENGAGED CITIZEN

ALEX KRIEGER

Architects take on and perform several important roles for society; they translate needs into physical form, create places, help illustrate futures, and advocate for quality, beauty and resilience in the environments in which we live. A role less often assumed — though no less significant to a human setting — is the architect as an engaged citizen of a particular urban milieu. At certain moments in their history, cities require the special engagement of their best architects and planners. Perhaps no better example of this exists than today's interaction between the City of New Orleans and the practice of Eskew+Dumez+Ripple (EDR).

That is not to suggest that the firm's ambitions or professional contributions are limited to local affairs, nor to civic advocacy alone. As this compelling volume of their work portrays, a number of cities and regions have benefited from the architectural talent and urban insights of EDR, as will other places in the future. But unlike many firms in practice today, to whom context is less important than range and opportunity, it is for their home base of New Orleans and its region that the passion to engage and excel is most evident.

The diversity of local work alone is remarkable. Schools and libraries, chapels and community centers, museums, cultural centers and centers for art, homes, apartment complexes and housing prototypes, environmental and research centers, hospitals, aquaria. This is the stuff of which cities are made!

Impressively, each of their projects is advanced in the spirit of what the noted architectural historian and critic, Kenneth Frampton, referred to as "critical regionalism." It is a modern vision deployed in support of geography, climate, resources and traditions. The result is an architecture rooted to place — substantially, not scenographically. Then there is the master plan to recapture civic connectivity and locate investment potential across 6 miles of Mississippi River bank, to which this essay will return. And, oh, not to overlook "Champions Square," the 2010 Super Bowl champs' expansive new arrival plaza and civic threshold at the foot of the Louisiana Superdome. And at another scale entirely, a whimsical proposal for an enticing little bathing pavilion, sadly not yet built.

As impressive as all of these are, neither the built nor conceptual projects represent the full measure of this firm's impact on New Orleans. Others in this volume speak more insightfully to the virtuosity of the firm's architectural production. The architecture is superb, though it may not constitute their most important long-term contribution to the urban future of New Orleans. How is it that an architect contributes more than his/her architecture to a place?

Ask almost anyone to identify an architect consistently engaged in the voluminous, arduous, acrimonious, emotion-sapping yet crucial public discussions about the rebuilding of New Orleans following Katrina, five years and counting, and Allen Eskew's name, the founding partner at EDR, will surface. He has been there: at all of the public ruminations and remains at the center of ongoing discussions. Not with the intention to seize advantage, spread theories, cajole or reprimand, but to help. Eskew believes that it is an obligation of citizenship to stay engaged, and to assist others about how to remain engaged as productively as possible. This has been his view across 35 years of living in New Orleans, not just the past five, as he constructed a career in which citizenship and professional values are seen as mutually supportive, not independent variables.

A long local residency has produced a passion for the architectural and cultural heritage of the Gulf region, absent of the sort of pining sentimentality frequently encountered in New Orleans and accompanied by stubborn resistance to change. Asked whether New Orleans should be rebuilt following Katrina Eskew quickly answers "absolutely," but adds, "Just rebuilding the stuff we had before would be a tragedy on top of a tragedy." It is the sort of comment that many residents find worrisome, as they are strongly determined to rebuild as before. Yet it is a necessary kind of observation if the city is to recover and thrive once more, and less threatening an idea coming from a neighbor so committed to that cause.

Among those who are perceptive about the future of New Orleans, rebuilding and recovery are understood as somewhat different goals. For Eskew and his colleagues at the firm, the latter is crucial, though locally perceived only as a consequence of rebuilding. Eskew understands that it is through recovery — of a tax base, an economy, of civic purpose — that prospects for reinvestment increase and sustainable rebuilding becomes far more likely.

Consider the role that EDR played and continues to play in the "Reinventing the Crescent: New Orleans Riverfront Plan." It is as a member of the planning and design team on this project that I was introduced to their complex engagement in the life of New Orleans, and gained full appreciation, indeed awe, for Allen Eskew's virtuosity as planner-cum-engaged citizen. The goals of the Reinventing the Crescent Plan are multiple yet strategically focused: to return the city to a positive interaction with its majestic river; to redeploy hundreds of underutilized acres of land along the river's banks for productive uses; to seize on the city building opportunities presented by the area's natural high ground; to attract new investment so crucial to the city's economic recovery; and to create a 6-mile corridor of public and civic spaces as befitting one of the world's great river cities. One can cite many officials, citizens, activists, planners and designers who have helped to advance the plan. Eskew is the first to rattle off the list. But unquestionably it has been his conviction and dogged pursuit of the project that has enabled it to proceed.

Eskew has led as manager/director of the large master planning team, as conduit to the city's leadership, as spokesman and mediator — for not all in the city support an initiative that may seem (erroneously) to move emphasis away from the rebuilding of damaged neighborhoods. As a tireless advocate for the cause, Eskew kept, and keeps, the initiative moving forward. Construction of the first phase began in the fall of 2010, and I am certain steady progress will continue until 2018, when the city will experience the 300th anniversary of its founding. It was Eskew, at a moment when the initiative seemed to be foundering and on the verge of abandonment, who helped reenergize local enthusiasm by suggesting how fitting it would be to celebrate the city's 300th anniversary at a reconstituted public riverfront, on the very geography responsible for the city's birth. The "Reinventing the Crescent" title for the riverfront project, itself a brilliant wordplay conjoining tradition, the evocation of the defining river crescent and progressive action in regards to its repurposing, captures the spirit of this urban design intervention.

Progressive action in New Orleans, as everywhere today, means an advanced degree of environmental stewardship, for which New Orleans historically has not been particularly well known. This is old hat at EDR, where a commitment to environmental issues precedes society's current turn to such matters. In 2010 *Architect* magazine recognized the firm as one of the top 25 architecture firms in the country, commending its "ecological commitment and design quality as much as profitability."

With built institutions such as the Aquarium of the Americas, the Shaw Center for the Arts in Baton Rouge, the Estuarine Habitats and Coastal Fisheries Center in Lafayette, master plans for Audubon's eastern New Orleans nature center, and projects such as the Make it Right Prototype House and the Global Green USA Sustainable Housing, the firm has the led the way among its regional peers. Partner Steve Dumez likes to remind clients that sustainability and green building design are everyday concerns at EDR, not exceptional ventures. He adds that the firm's goal is not to proselytize but to demonstrate actual long-term economic value resulting from environmentally based design decisions. Amid the famously fragile ecosystems of the Gulf, such a professional mindset seems responsible. Indeed, it is essential. Of course, EDR's commitment to a place, its stewardship and renewal, is itself a fundamental strategy of sustainability. Sustain, build upon, creatively evolve that which is already here, Eskew and his colleagues say. Commit to the energy long embedded in this place.

It seems almost quaint these days to be so locally attached. Amid today's intellectual posturing and market seeking, the very idea of committing to, patiently learning from and slowly transforming a place seems un-entrepreneurial, if not naïve. Who has the time?

Today's successful architect, it seems, must participate on an expansive stage, follow global trends and seek broad acclaim as a means to attain influence. Fame must be acquired precociously and used. The architect must perform, leaving precious little time for local affairs or patient searches. That has not been the EDR way, and their success warrants considerable reflection. Will not New Orleans' future, along with that of many American cities, depend in part on others emulating the EDR version of the "think globally, act locally" philosophy? During prior epochs, American Manifest Destiny meant moving on, to the West or to the "burbs." For the staff at EDR in the 21st century, it means to stay, nurture, improve.

One can think of a handful of instances, mostly historical, when a design firm and its leadership have been so powerfully connected to and contributed so essentially to one place. Charles Bulfinch at the beginning of the 19th century in post-colonial Boston. Burnham and Root towards the turn from the 19th to the 20th centuries in Chicago. Ed Bacon in mid-20th century Philadelphia, and his often maligned administrator counterpart in New York, Robert Moses. I make such comparisons with considerable trepidation. It is not my intention to inflate the importance of this studio, and surely all three — Allen Eskew, Steve Dumez and Mark Ripple — would be quite uncomfortable and resist such comparisons. The problem is that there are few comparables to today's EDR.

Eskew+Dumez+Ripple is a seminal professional organization; a gathering of talented architects, insightful planners, committed urban activists, environmental stewards and citizens fully engaged in the welfare of their home domain. Constructive collaboration, not heroic visioning or loud posturing/cajoling constitutes their business model. Among the many role models to which tomorrow's architects might aspire, with which to plan for a more healthy and sustainable urban future, that of engaged citizen must rank high.

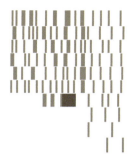   

# 930 POYDRAS RESIDENTIAL TOWER

NEW ORLEANS, LOUISIANA

This 21-floor mixed-use residential project is designed to re-imagine the typically horizontal condition of New Orleans' dense French Quarter blocks as a vertical condition. The program includes 250 residential apartments above a 500-car garage, and is organized to create a communal amenity floor at the ninth floor level — reinterpreting the courtyard housing typology for urban, high-rise living. At this raised "courtyard" level, shuttle elevators transfer from garage to tower in order to promote opportunities for residents to cross paths with one another in a shared, communal space as opposed to the typical, introverted collection of experiences found in most high-rise residential developments.

As a means to recreate the social interaction found in the courtyards of the city's historic quarter, the design consolidates all tenant amenities at the ninth-floor level in order to condense their programmatic force. Anchoring this level is the "sky lobby," a dramatic glass box that cantilevers out from the façade and offers spectacular views of the downtown skyline. This double-height lounge serves as an extension of the tenant's living spaces, with coffee bar and movie screening lounge set among informal groupings of furniture. Outside the sky lobby is an expansive pool deck, with a tiered bleacher rising from the pool to a sunning platform at its top. Tucked beneath these bleachers is the facility's fitness center. A series of townhomes along the south side — with front-door access directly off the pool deck — create an architectural edge and produce the effect of a ground-level courtyard on the garage rooftop.

Departing from the oppressive monotony of the commercial office towers surrounding it, the design of the exterior envelope incorporates a highly articulated metal panel and glass-patterned façade. This approach allows for a higher percentage of glazing at the upper residential floors with a minimal amount of glass at the garage provided in order to maintain a seamless, while animated, composition. The proportion of windows and insulated metal panels are extended vertically over two floors, with vertical joints in the panels shifted a half module each repeat, giving the building a non-hierarchical pattern that reinforces the appearance of a monolithic skin.

The project site is located on the primary commercial corridor of the city, in close proximity to a number of urban parks, central business district offices, the downtown medical district, universities, urban shopping districts and entertainment venues. The Louisiana Superdome, the Mississippi riverfront, the entire central business district and the French Quarter are all within a 1-mile radius of the project.

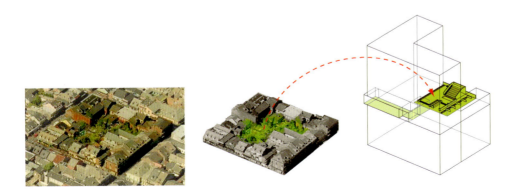

Taking its inspiration from the social interaction typically found in the shared space of French Quarter courtyards, the design consolidates all tenant amenities at the ninth floor. Shuttle elevators transfer residents from garage to apartments at this level, creating opportunities for chance interaction among residents and promoting community in what is typically an introverted housing type.

APARTMENTS

COMMON AREAS

PARKING

RETAIL

COURTYARD
TOWNHOUSES     POOL DECK

SKY LOBBY    POOL DECK    FITNESS ROOM

Section Diagram Showing Program Distribution

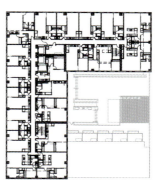

Typical Residential Floor

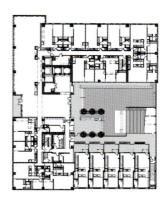

Ninth Floor

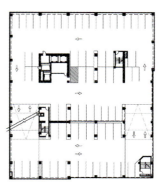

Typical Parking Floor

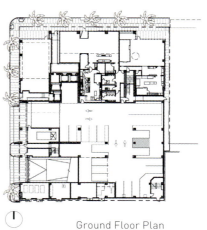

Ground Floor Plan

The fitness room for residents is located below bleacher
seating that steps down to the pool.

Artwork by Jonathan Ferrara, "Overtopped (Midnight)"

The building meets the street with a collection of retail units — a pizzeria, juice bar and upscale restaurant/lounge — enlivening the street for residents and the community. The sidewalk is covered with a projected awning, which folds the metal skin of the façade up off the ground to provide weather protection across the entire retail street frontage.

| | |
|---|---|
| Client | Gibbs Development, LLC |
| Architect of Record | Eskew+Dumez+Ripple |
| Project Team | Steve Dumez, Charles Hite, Jack Sawyer, Jose Alvarez, |
| | Wendy Kerrigan, Robert Kleinpeter, Shawn Préau, |
| | Cynthia Dubberley, Magen R. Gladden |
| General Contractor | Gibbs Construction Company |
| Structural Engineer | Morphy Makofsky, Inc. |
| Mechanical Engineer | Mechanical Construction Co. (Design Build) |
| Electrical Engineer | Canzoneri & Associates (Design Build) |
| Civil Engineer | Morphy Makofsky, Inc. |
| Geotechnical Engineer | Eustis Engineering |
| MEP Engineer | Moses Engineers (Retail Space Only) |
| Photographer | Timothy Hursley |

## LOUISIANA IMMERSIVE
## TECHNOLOGIES ENTERPRISE
LAFAYETTE, LOUISIANA

A cooperative endeavor between the Lafayette Economic Development Authority and the University of Louisiana, Lafayette, the Louisiana Immersive Technology Enterprise (LITE) was conceived as an economic generator for the greater Lafayette region. The project provides unprecedented research and development opportunities utilizing computer visualization technologies for a wide range of potential leasing clients — from oil and gas exploration companies to university researchers.

LITE includes incubator office space for several data technology companies, along with a variety of high-performance immersion environments including a 200-seat auditorium, two multi-purpose conference rooms and a 3-D visualization cube (or CAVE). The cube is the first total immersion environment of its kind in the region, and one of only a handful in the nation.

In order to call attention to the high-performance technology contained within, the client requested that the cube be featured as a prominent visual element within the design. To accomplish this goal, the self-contained cube is sheathed with an outer skin of translucent glass. The interstitial space between the glass envelope and the interior cube is illuminated at night, providing an ethereal glow of colored light.

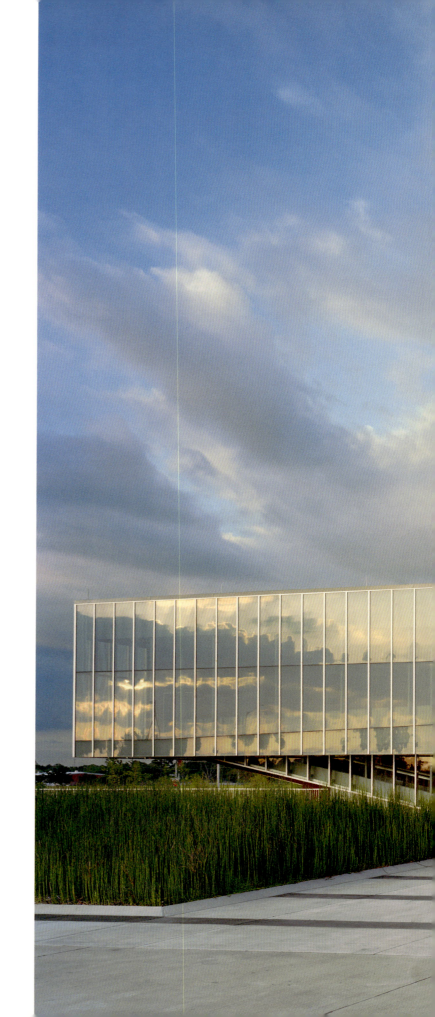

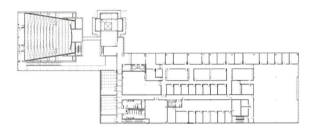

Second Floor Plan

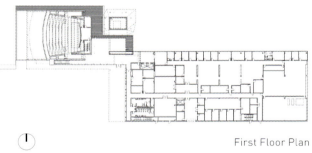

First Floor Plan

The 3D visualization cube, Total Immersion Space (TIS), allows multiple users to be completely immersed in a virtual environment. The TIS is an advanced 10' x 10', six-sided cube using multiple projectors in a motion-tracking environment.

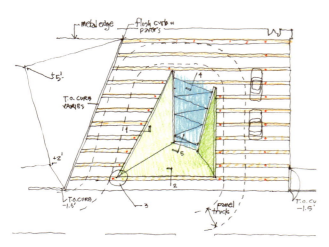

Sketch of Entry Court / Fountain

| | |
|---|---|
| Client | Lafayette Economic Development Authority |
| Architect of Record | Eskew+Dumez+Ripple / Guidry Beazley Architects, A Joint Venture |
| Project Team | Steve Dumez, R. Allen Eskew, Nick Marshall, Alan Lewis, Jaime Ramiro Diaz, Blaise Durio, Amanda Rivera, Robert Kleinpeter, Shannon Downey Tufts, Kiyomi Troemner |
| General Contractor | J.B. Mouton, Inc. |
| Landscape Architect | Jon Emerson & Associates, Inc. |
| Structural Engineer | Bellard and Associates |
| MEP Engineer | Associated Design Group |
| Visualization Systems | Visual Acuity |
| Communication/IT Design | Global Data Systems |
| Fountain Design | Fountain People, Inc. |
| Photographer | Timothy Hursley |

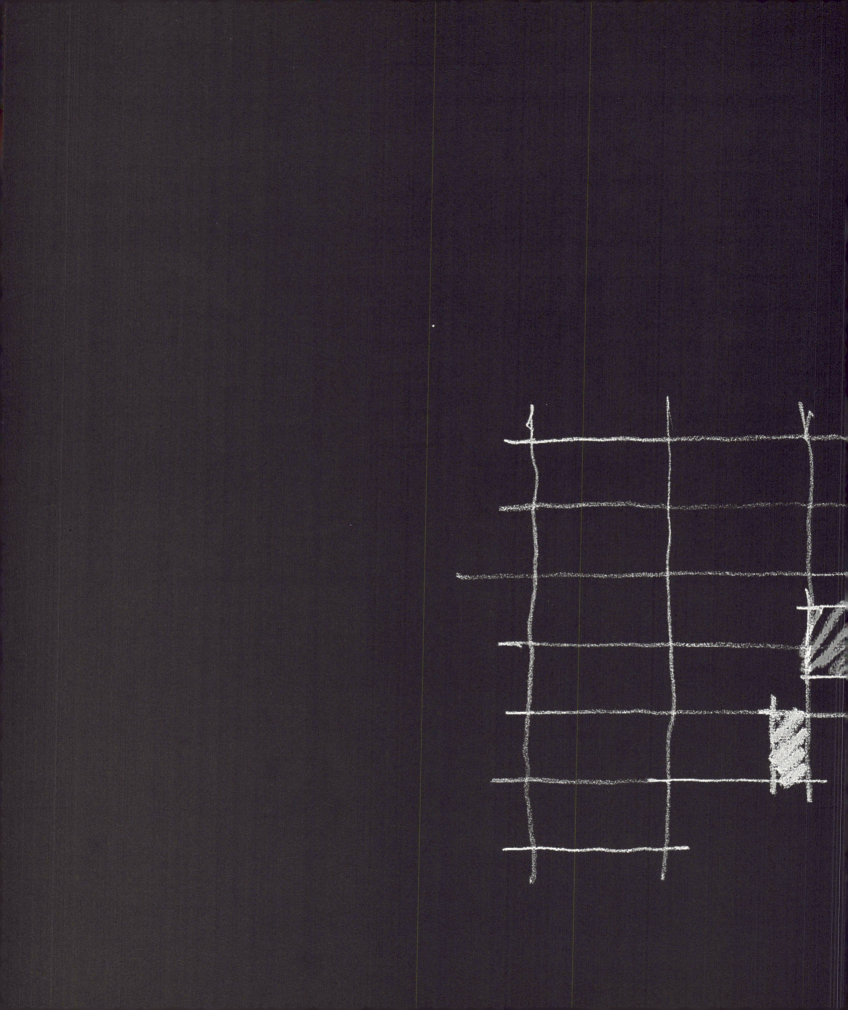

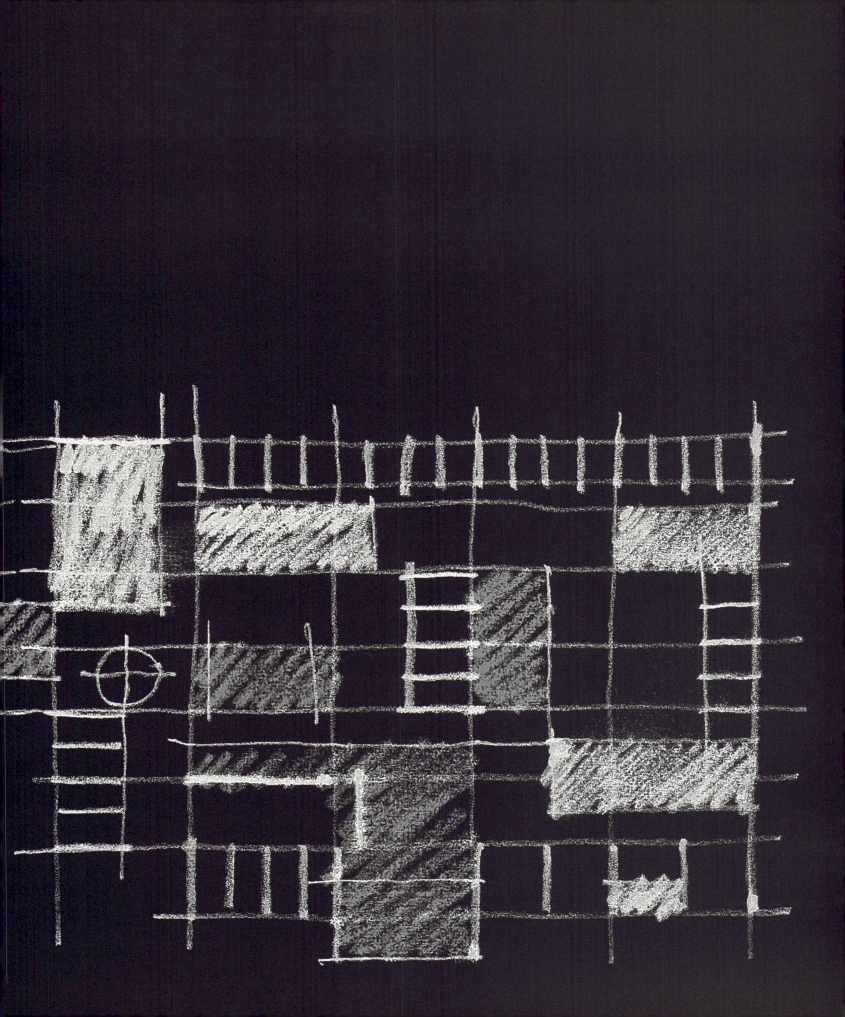

## LAMAR ADVERTISING
## CORPORATE HEADQUARTERS
BATON ROUGE, LOUISIANA

This design of a new workplace for a billboard advertising company's corporate headquarters is a reaction against the standard office environment. People require interaction in today's workplace — they go to work to meet and collaborate, to brainstorm, to do research, to do a whole range of activities they don't necessarily think of as "work" in the traditional sense of the word. Much of what we observe in creative environments is informal interaction in settings not typical or "traditional," such as chance meetings in corridors or conversations around the coffee pot. Our design proposal is structured to reinforce this culture of openness.

To accomplish this goal, we radically altered the internal configuration of a 1970s-era data center while leaving the exterior essentially unchanged. The existing building had a very large floor plate along with narrow windows with limited views to the outside. To counteract this condition, our proposal introduces an outdoor court that penetrates to the second floor of the building — a garden "room" that introduces a captured landscape in the middle of the office environment.

Elsewhere in the design, additional structure is removed to connect the various floors into one communicating whole — reinforcing the culture and identity of the company as a singular creative community. Primary among these interventions is a bleacher/stair adjacent to the company café. Here, the entire office staff can congregate for company-wide announcements or group presentations, watch movies, nor sporting events (or even advertisements) on the digital "billboard" or simply hang out in a new Lamar "town square."

Front Elevation

New Headquarters          Existing Headquarters

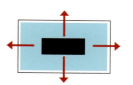 Site Aerial

By removing structural bays of the large floor plate of the former data center, the design transforms Lamar's office environment from one externally oriented to one more inwardly focused.

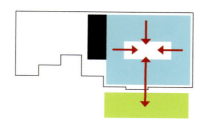

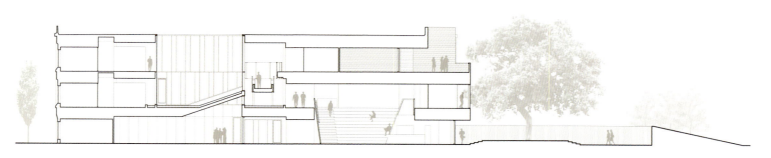

Building Section

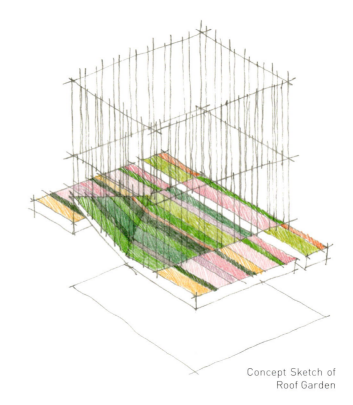

Concept Sketch of
Roof Garden

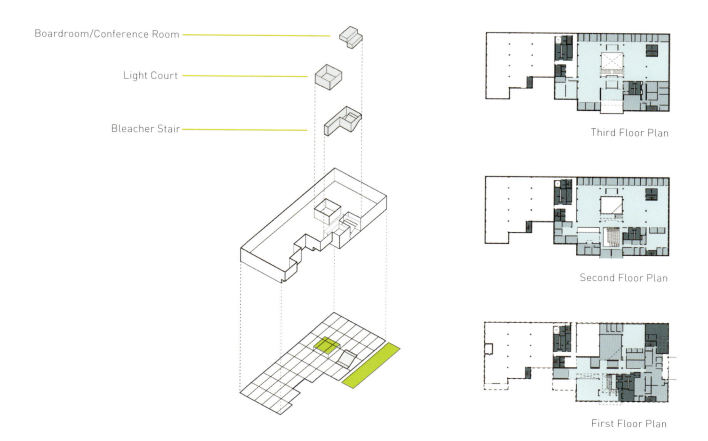

Boardroom/Conference Room

Light Court

Bleacher Stair

Third Floor Plan

Second Floor Plan

First Floor Plan

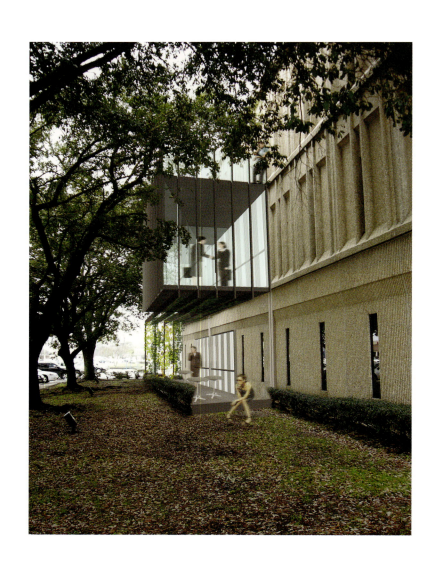

| | |
|---|---|
| Client | Lamar Advertising Company |
| Architect of Record | Eskew+Dumez+Ripple . |
| Project Team | Steve Dumez, Tracy Lea, Thaddeus Zarse, Michael Keller, |
| | Marty McElveen, Isaac Williams, Mark Reynolds, |
| | Jessica Stumpf, Robert Kleinpeter |
| General Contractor | Bouquet & LeBlanc, Inc. |
| Landscape Architect | Spackman, Mossop + Michaels |
| Structural Engineer | Fox-Nesbit Engineering, LLC |
| MEP Engineer | Henderson Engineers, Inc. |
| Civil Engineer | Fox-Nesbit Engineering, LLC |

## U.S. FISH & WILDLIFE
## FISH TECHNOLOGY CENTER

BOZEMAN, MONTANA

This new research center supports U.S. Fish and Wildlife Service studies on fish reproduction, nutrition and contaminants, as well as fish physiology and therapeutic drug research. The facility includes a new high-performance research laboratory and administration headquarters, which centralizes USFWS fish technology center staff into a single structure. A small interpretive center component promotes public outreach and environmental education opportunities, as well as providing visitors the opportunity to orient themselves to the Fish Technology Center mission and site before embarking on a self-guided tour of the grounds.

Operationally, the laboratory component is programmed to maintain 24/7 operations, while the administrative program operates on a conventional eight-hour weekday schedule. In addition, security considerations require a clear separation of uses along similar lines. For this reason, the design is organized into two discrete wings with limited, controlled access to the research laboratories and public access to the administrative center.

The design differentiates between administrative center and laboratory by cladding the former in wood (along with researchers' offices) and the latter in aluminum panels. These material selections reinforce the vernacular and industrial setting of the immediate region. Wood siding is Western Red Cedar, a rapidly renewable species native to the Northern Rockies, and is regionally harvested and milled. The aluminum roof and wall panels are a recyclable material that minimizes waste to landfill.

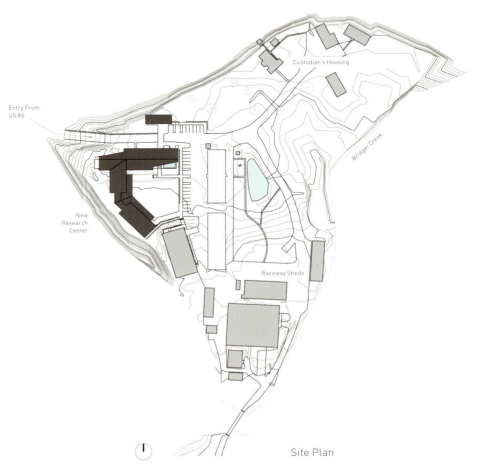

Entry From
US 86

Custodian's Housing

New
Research
Center

Bridger Creek

Raceway Sheds

Site Plan

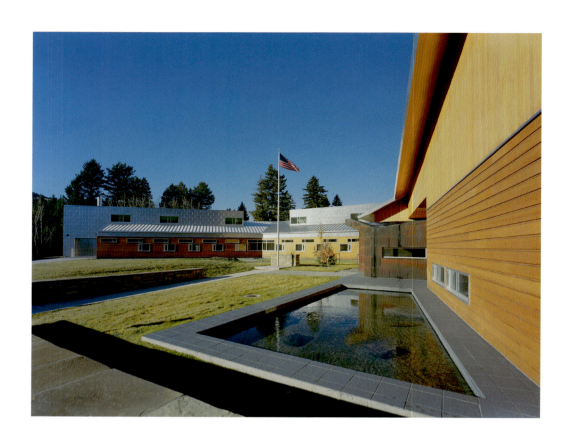

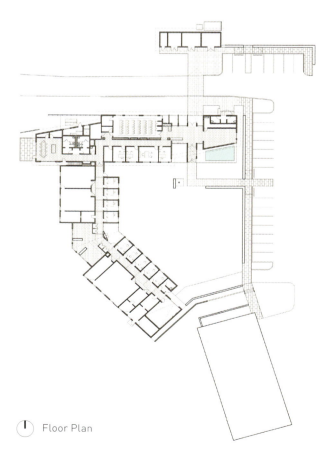

1 Floor Plan

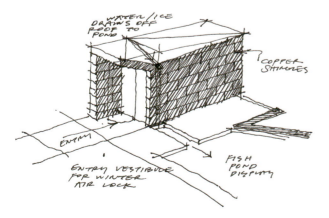

The administrative lobby is designed to be visually open and accessible, with separate entries to the north and the south from visitor and staff parking areas. The design addresses the severe Montana winter climate by enabling the north (visitor) entry to the lobby to be shuttered throughout the winter months by means of operable, insulated panels. During this period, visitors and staff are redirected to the south lobby entry, where a copper-clad vestibule provides an air-lock for winter use.

| | |
|---|---|
| Client | U.S. Fish and Wildlife Service |
| Architect of Record | Eskew+Dumez+Ripple / Guidry Beazley Architects, A Joint Venture |
| Project Team | R. Allen Eskew, Steve Dumez, Charles Hite, Nick Marshall, Shannon Downey Tufts, Jose Alvarez, Robert Kleinpeter, Kiyomi Troemner, Kevin Morris |
| General Contractor | Dick Anderson Construction |
| Structural Engineer | McKee & Deville Consulting Engineers, Inc. |
| MEP Engineer | Associated Design Group, Inc. |
| Civil Engineer | Sellards & Griggs, Inc. |
| Laboratory Consultant | Earl Walls Associates |
| Photographer | Timothy Hursley |

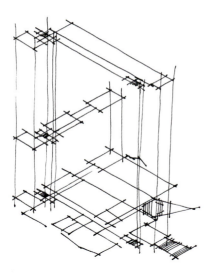

## INTERNATIONAL GAME FISH ASSOCIATION HALL OF FAME & MUSEUM
FORT LAUDERDALE, FLORIDA

The International Game Fish Association (IGFA) was established in 1939 for the initial purpose of maintaining sport fishing world records, and later expanded to address emerging issues of species conservation, education and advocacy. This hall of fame and museum in Fort Lauderdale was conceived in 1996 to house the IGFA's world headquarters, to create a public attraction which honored the legends of sport fishing, and to educate the public about the history, science and sport of recreational fishing.

Carefully sited in a previously undeveloped parcel adjacent to heavily traveled Interstate-95, the facility was conceived as an object surrounded and influenced by water — a large reflecting pond to the south, a boat dock to the east, interpretive wetlands exhibit to the north and a water feature at the entrance. The building envelope subtly expresses the dual language of "fish" as well as "fishing" in materiality, texture and pattern. The abundant use of stainless steel, white plaster and sculpted forms evokes the language of sleek sport fishing vessels; simultaneously, the staggered pattern of stainless wall panels reflected in the light of the surrounding pond evokes the shimmering iridescent qualities of fish emerging from the water. The most prominent element in the composition is a large triangular "fin," housing a 100-seat movie theater and serving as the iconic marker to those passing by on I-95. At the base of the fin, operable overhead doors allow theater viewers to witness an interactive water jet feature through the glazed opening at the show's end.

Numerous exterior building features support the IGFA mission while sensitively reflecting the south Florida environment. Near the entrance, the building profile is sculpted to create an amphitheater for use as an outdoor continuing education venue. At the interpretive wetlands, constructed from the carcass of a reclaimed wastewater pond, visitors are guided through a series of freshwater exhibits including native fish, amphibians and flora.

At the public exhibit areas, the sport fishing message is reinforced by subtle architectural features that are integral to and complement the exhibits. At the lobby, an angular ceiling of wood slats suggests the underside of a boat bottom which, combined with subtle backlighting and a suspended cluster of metal fish shapes, evokes an underwater, submerged experience. Coquina stone containing fossilized shellfish remains lines the walls of major public spaces, leaving a subtle impression on the visitor. The total effect is of a figurative submersion, intended to take the visitor from the human world above to the marine world below.

At the second floor, a glass-enclosed library with more than 12,000 volumes offers educational opportunities and quiet research spaces, as well as views to the wetlands beyond.

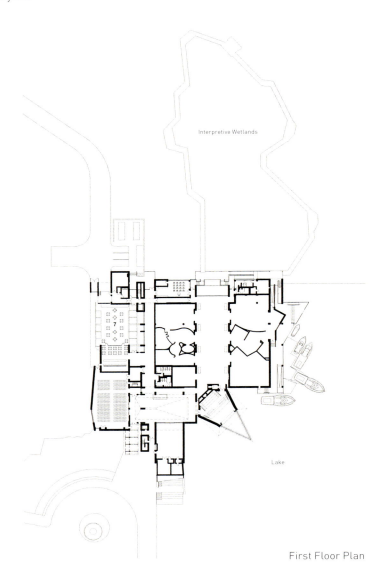

Interpretive Wetlands

Lake

First Floor Plan

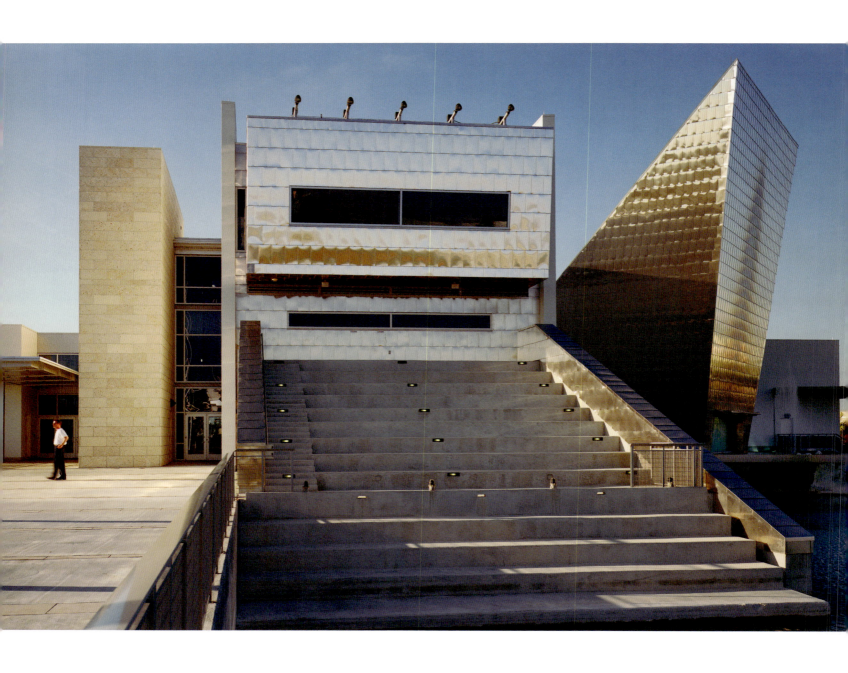

At courtyards, brise soleil elements and palm trees serve to soften harsh midday sun and create livable outdoor environments.

A central "Hall of Greats" contains world record mounts of every species IGFA maintains records for, and provides access to each of the six focus galleries.

| | |
|---|---|
| Client | International Game Fish Association |
| Architect of Record | Eskew+Dumez+Ripple |
| Project Team | Mark Ripple, R. Allen Eskew, Steve Dumez, Tracy Lea, |
| | Gabriel Smith, B.J. Siegel, Robert Kleinpeter, Nick Marshall, |
| | John Anderson, Gary Hoffman, Debra Warner, Jennifer Calla, |
| | Steve Dangermond |
| Structural Engineer | Jenkins & Charland, Inc. |
| MEP Engineer | Blum Consulting Engineers, Inc. |
| Landscape Architect | Ekistics Design Studio, Craven Thompson & Associates, Inc. |
| Civil Engineer | Williams Engineering, Inc. |
| Exhibit Designer | Gerard Hilferty & Associates |
| General Contractor | Centex-Rooney Construction Co. |
| Interpretive Planner | Word Craft |
| Economic Feasibility | Harrison Price Company |
| Lighting Design | Cline Bettridge Bernstein Lighting Design, Inc. |
| Film Production | Donna Lawrence Productions, Inc. |
| Fountain Design | Wet Design |
| Exhibit Lighting Design | Yeager Design |
| Acoustical Engineer | Bonner Associates |
| Photographer | Timothy Hursley |

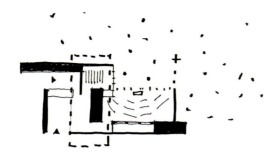

## ST. MARTHA CATHOLIC CHURCH

HARVEY, LOUISIANA

This Roman Catholic Church — replacing an existing worship space that has been converted to a multipurpose Parish Hall — was designed through a series of interactive, hands-on workshops with the entire church congregation. Over 150 parishioners participated in six workshops over a four-month period, which allowed all participants to directly contribute to the ultimate building design and worship configuration.

The church is sited in the middle of a suburban neighborhood, surrounded by the rear yards of adjacent single-family residences. The new worship space is strategically located at the center of the church property adjacent to a large grove of trees, engaging the existing landscape to connect the church to nature. Future plans envision this tree grove as an expanded worship space with a meditation walk containing an outdoor stations of the cross.

A layered planning organization relates the church front (neighborhood/approach) to the everyday, in contrast to the rear (nature/repose) as more hallowed. This duality is reinforced by the material qualities of the building. Brick masonry is used for gathering spaces at the church entry, which grounds the project to its earthly, physical site. Alternately, metal wall panels clad the worship space with a lighter, more ephemeral material. The church tower — which doubles as a campanile — weaves both materials together in a symbolic knitting of sacred and secular to visually assert the church's public presence from a distance.

The campanile has an internal presence as well, with tall vertical windows allowing natural light to enter the high volume of the day chapel located within the tower's base. The soaring interior gives the day chapel a dramatic spaciousness less present in the more intimately scaled main sanctuary, reflecting a desire expressed by the congregation through the workshop process.

A unique feature of the design resulted from the need to satisfy all stormwater retention on site. The roof of the worship space is inverted to serve as a collector, sloping to a single location where an over-scaled scupper deposits rainwater into a large retention pond. This feature is made visible to the congregation by means of a large window above the altar, allowing worshippers the ability to experience this episodic event connecting earth and sky.

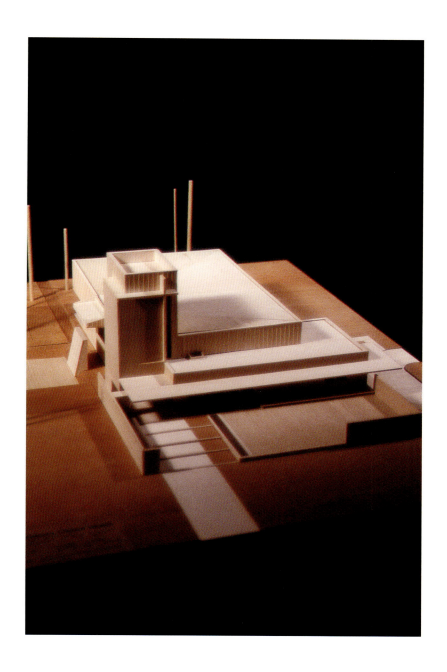

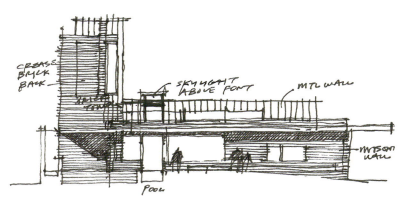

Entry Elevation Sketch

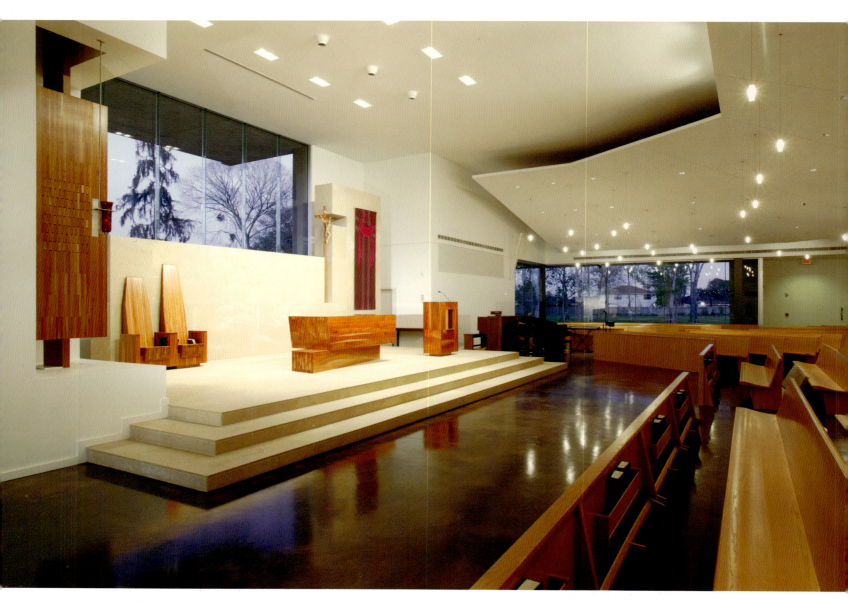

The congregation participated in a series of hands-on workshops in the planning of the main worship space. The plans were each presented and discussed for their various merits. The final floor plan for the sanctuary was crafted to ensure that the liturgical elements are carefully arranged to provide a close relationship with the priest, the congregation and the liturgy.

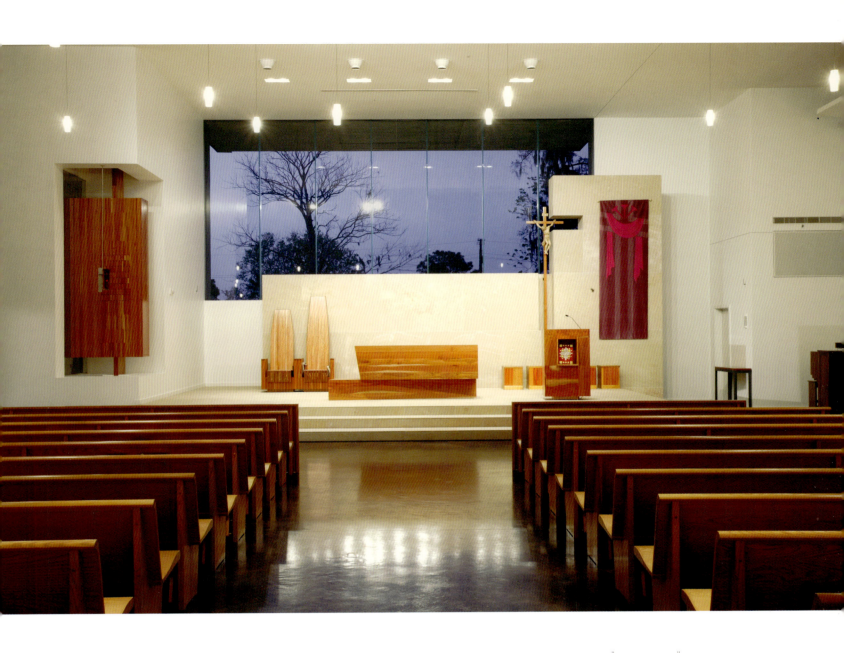

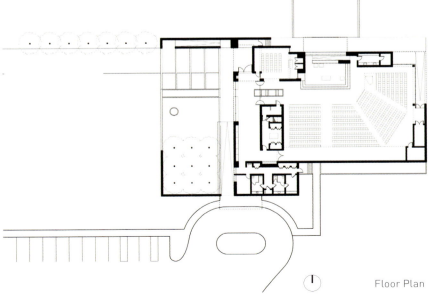

Floor Plan

The custom-fabricated liturgical elements include the pulpit, the altar, the tabernacle, and the presider's and deacons' chairs — all milled from cherrywood plank.

The 50-seat day chapel occupies the base of the entry tower campanile, where the full volume of the tower floods the chapel with daylight.

| | |
|---|---|
| Client | The Archdiocese of New Orleans |
| Architect of Record | Eskew+Dumez+Ripple |
| Project Team | Steve Dumez, R. Allen Eskew, Charles Hite, Byron Mouton, Robert Kleinpeter, Rick Dupont, Vicki Smith, Jose Alvarez, Kurt Hagstette, Tracy Lea |
| General Contractor | F. H. Myers Construction Company |
| Structural Engineer | McKee & Deville Consulting Engineers, Inc. |
| MEP Engineer | Smith Seckman Reid, Inc. |
| Civil Engineer | Dufrene Surveying and Engineering |
| Geotechnical Engineer | Eustis Engineering Company |
| Photographer | Timothy Hursley |

FILTER
SOUTH
LIGHT

VIEW

COUR

KIDS
CORNER

GARD
COU

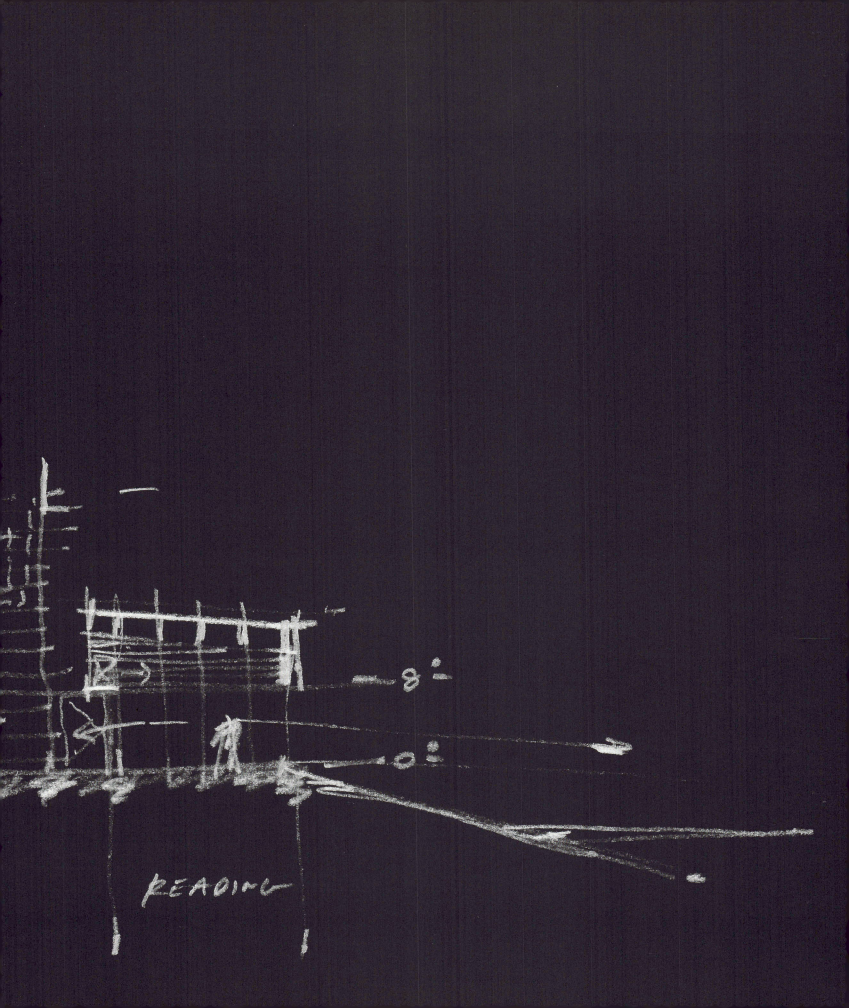

# ROSA F. KELLER LIBRARY
# & COMMUNITY CENTER

NEW ORLEANS, LOUISIANA

This branch library in the Broadmoor neighborhood of New Orleans was severely flooded by levee breaks attributed to Hurricane Katrina. The library was composed of two buildings joined together to function as one. The first is a historically significant two-story bungalow built as a residence in 1917. The second building, a 1993 addition to the original house, was designed specifically to function as a library and contained the main reading room and stock areas.

The new library entails the complete restoration of the original residence, converting it into a neighborhood community center. A new library wing replaces the old library and is designed so that the two buildings can function as a single unit or independent of one another, providing programmatic flexibility for a variety of users.

A new lobby provides a minimal link between the two buildings and a transition between the architecture of old and new. The library program is organized around a captured courtyard that acts as a garden respite for library users and provides natural light to the center of the building. Program components of reading room, circulation, book stacks and children's room all pinwheel around this outdoor court. The wood glue lam structure is designed to reveal this pinwheel organization and helps define independent program uses as it rises in scale from the library entry to a high point containing the mechanical core.

WALKER WE...
EUDORA WE...
FLANNERY O'CONNE...
HARPER LEE
ROBERT PENN WARR...
MARGARET MITCHE...
WILLIAM FAUL...

Building Section

North Elevation

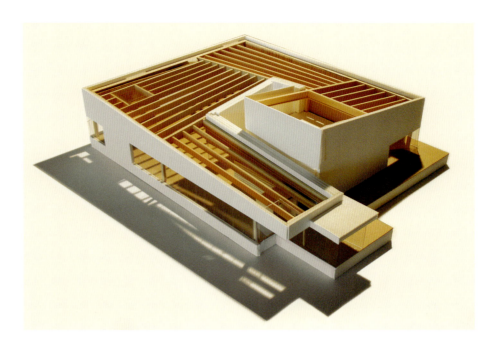

Study Model

Site/Program Organization

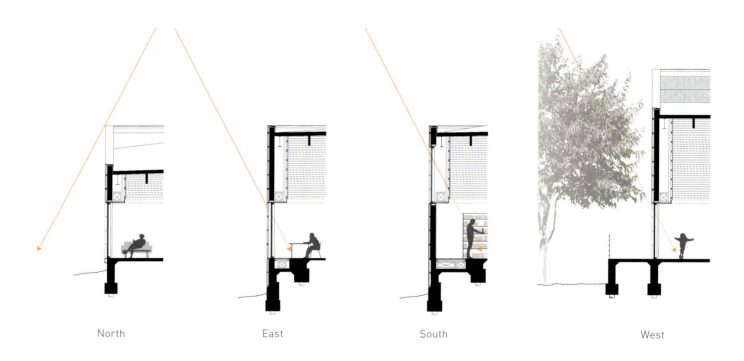

North                East              South             West

| | |
|---:|:---|
| Client | City of New Orleans, New Orleans Public Library |
| Architect of Record | Eskew+Dumez+Ripple |
| Project Team | R. Allen Eskew, Steve Dumez, Kurt Hagstette, Jason Richards, |
| | David Demsey, Rick Dupont, Robert Kleinpeter |
| General Contractor | Ryan Gootee General Contractors |
| Landscape Architect | Spackman, Mossop + Michaels |
| Structural Engineer | Kulkarni Consultants |
| MEP Engineer | Lucien T. Vivien & Associates |
| Civil Engineer | Kulkarni Consultants |
| Geotechnical Engineer | Professional Services Industries, Inc. |

# THE SPIRIT OF PLACE

LAWRENCE SCARPA

History and tradition run deep in the South, but even deeper in New Orleans. Food, music, people, community and folklore make up a gumbo of life that is so unique to the city that its history has become the guide to the present. Rarely has contemporary architecture found a way to enhance the true character and life of this unique city.

Practicing contemporary architecture in a place so deeply rooted in its tradition is difficult. But when you couple the city's love of its history with a climate that literally eats buildings faster than a good crawfish pie, the odds are not good that a firm that practices contemporary architecture has any chance of survival. Yet when you visit the studio of Eskew+Dumez+Ripple, it becomes immediately clear why they have been so successful.

Upon arrival at the studio, you immediately sense that there is something special here, something deeply rooted in the history and culture of the city. There is also something refreshing, exciting and new. Located on the 31st floor of an office building high above New Orleans overlooking the French Quarter, it is almost as if the studio is the guardian of the city, watching, observing and learning, like parents awaiting the birth of their newborn child. The history of the past seems to be illuminating the history of the present and future buildings yet to be born.

Just as Carlo Scarpa, the great Italian master of modern architecture, had a deep passion and understanding of history, the principals at Eskew+Dumez+Ripple share a similar respect for their regional culture and tradition. And, like Scarpa before them, Allen Eskew, Steve Dumez and Mark Ripple grew up in the place where they practice, embracing local tradition as well

as contemporary culture in a way that has become refreshingly beautiful, that feels both familiar and unfamiliar all at the same time. As Robert Venturi wrote in his book *Complexity and Contradiction*, "A familiar thing seen in an unfamiliar way becomes both perceptually old and new." This concept is deeply rooted in the work of Eskew+Dumez+Ripple.

I remember visiting the then recently completed Louisiana State Museum in downtown Baton Rouge, Louisiana for the first time and being immediately struck by the shiny perforated metal façade. It was unlike any other building I had seen in the South. As I approached the building to explore it more closely, I began to understand the role that the metal "screen" played, and its important relationship to the history of the region. Not unlike the shutters of a traditional Louisiana home, so commonly found in the South, the perforated metal acts like a breathable skin, shading the core of the building, allowing filtered light, air and views to pass through it, while simultaneously protecting the building from the unforgiving climate. The metal skin is both a clear response to the harsh climate of the region and a reference to history. The building possesses a unique, stimulating quality of natural light, respecting history while reflecting upon contemporary culture.

I entered the building via the main entry, a more than 30-foot-high covered porch surrounded by the perforated metal skin. Light-filled and beautifully detailed, the porch is impressive; the space is embracing. It is a shelter that holds and protects you, opening to the north and positioned on axis with the state capitol building of Louisiana. To view the Capitol from the entry porch of the museum is breathtaking. The two buildings seem to collapse together and fuse into one structure. In the long reflecting pool located under the porch, the reflection of the Capitol appears in the pool as a constant dreamlike reminder that the people, state history and contemporary culture all belong together. In contrast to traditional buildings, this place does more with less. The space provokes a kind of indelible wonder while still affording traditional values to the people who visit.

At the Paul and Lulu Hilliard University Art Museum in Lafayette, Louisiana, for example, Eskew+Dumez+Ripple faced a design challenge in placing a contemporary art museum within the context of a traditional Louisiana plantation house. Contrasting with its *antebellum* predecessor, but also paying homage to it, the museum respects its neighbor while making a stand for contemporary culture. As one approaches, the building is hardly noticeable. A simple precast concrete wall flanks the existing structure, matching its stucco façade in color and texture. But as you move toward the main entry, so cleverly located around the corner on the façade adjacent to, and directly across from the historic structure, something unique and captivating begins to unfold. The second floor of the building exterior is composed of a specially coated reflective glass curtain wall, which overhangs the more transparent glass on the first floor. As a result, the lower floor disappears while the upper floor floats above the site and creates a reflective backdrop to the historic structure. The new building appears to levitate above the site, while the historic structure feels solid and grounded to the earth. This illusion enhances the buildings, giving them a collective strength that neither building could possess individually.

Like the body of Eskew+Dumez+Ripple's work, the boundary between the new and old is blurred. Even though 30 feet separate the two structures, they perceptually merge into each other. Depending on the hour of the day or viewing angle, the glass alternates between being reflective and transparent. This combination of reflecting and absorbing the historic building engages the users, heightens their sense of awareness and brings a sense of vitality to the place. From the interior the viewer can see the rhythm of the glass curtain wall in front of the heavy columns of the antebellum house. They appear to be dancing together as one moves along the interior space of the museum. Color lighting reinforces this relationship — deep blue for the new building and crisp white for the existing structure. Every feature of the building is multivalent and rich with meaning— performing several roles for functional, formal and experiential effect. Like an inseparable bond between two lovers, it is hard to imagine these two buildings without each other. This marriage of the old and new, this respect for history while bringing something entirely new and exciting to the art museum campus, makes this building inseparable from the history of the region. This concept exemplifies the true genius of the firm.

Eskew+Dumez+Ripple is interested in how buildings fit into society, how people fit into buildings and how to bring all of this together for the public good. Every detail is considered with a modernist restraint and a concern for the neighbor. They have positioned themselves in the field of architecture as potent form seekers and as socially responsive practitioners, a combination not easily or often found. Comfortable with aesthetic, practical, political and functional issues, they have mapped an architectural path that is as didactic as it is successful.

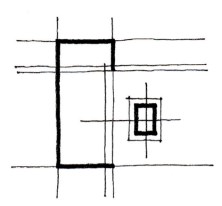

## PAUL AND LULU HILLIARD UNIVERSITY ART MUSEUM
LAFAYETTE, LOUISIANA

Situated adjacent to the original 1967 University Art Museum (a replica of an antebellum plantation home designed by noted Louisiana architect A. Hays Town) this new museum building serves as a backdrop to the original and defines the edge of a new sculpture garden and plaza. The program includes lobby and public spaces, permanent collection and changing exhibit galleries, museum offices, art storage and support spaces.

Conceived of as a tightly wrapped solid, the construction module of the new museum responds to the structural rhythm of the original building while clearly departing in material and treatment. The new building's glass façade hovers above visitors entering the museum, reflecting in its surface the existing Hays Town Building and live oaks of the surrounding sculpture gardens. Depending on position and time of day, the glass façade oscillates between opaque and transparent, and at night is rendered in a deep blue light through the use of cold cathode tubes located above perforated metal ceilings.

Internally, the building spatially unfolds as the visitor moves through a series of sky-lit spaces punctuated by vertical shafts that penetrate the lobby and atrium gallery. A simple planning organization clearly differentiates art spaces from support spaces. To further assist with visitor orientation, a common public area is provided along the entire face of the second floor, where the expansive glass façade allows uninterrupted views back to the Hays Town Building, plaza fountain and sculpture garden.

The design approach strategically focuses construction dollars to achieve the greatest design impact. Twin glass façades occupy a mere 10-foot depth along the face of the building, while the remainder of the project utilizes simple, straightforward construction in order to leverage a modest construction budget to maximum effect.

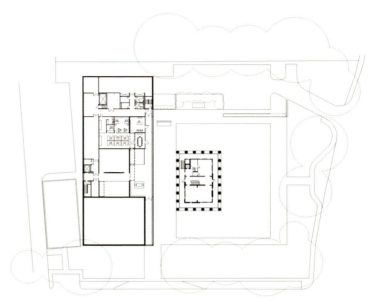

Second Floor Plan

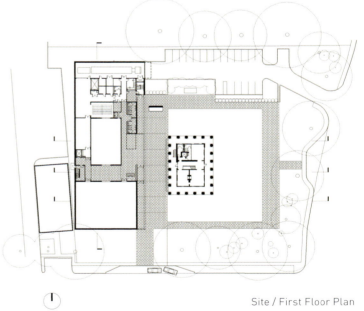

Site / First Floor Plan

"Darryl Pottorf: A Perspective"

Cross Section

Cross Section

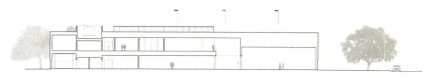

Longitudinal Section

The 5,000-square-foot Changing Exhibit Gallery was designed for maximum flexibility to accommodate various configurations for a wide range of art. These photographs depict the main Changing Exhibit Gallery showcasing a range of artists and creative mediums: at left is shown "Scenarios and Short Stories", by Robert Rauschenberg; at top is "Horses", by Deborah Butterfield; and directly above is "Helga: An Intimate Study", by Andrew Wyeth.

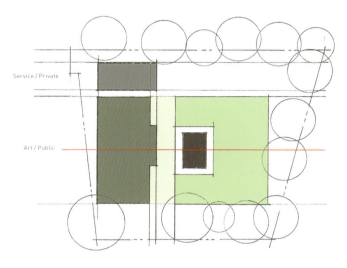

Service / Private

Art / Public

Site Organization

| | |
|---|---|
| Client | University of Louisiana at Lafayette Foundation |
| Architect of Record | Eskew+Dumez+Ripple |
| Project Team | R. Allen Eskew, Steve Dumez, Charles Hite, Gabriel Smith, |
| | Vincent Bandy, Robert Kleinpeter, Shannon Downey Tufts, |
| | Jose Alvarez, Kurt Hagstette, Nick Marshall, |
| | Sebastian Salvado, Kevin Morris |
| General Contractor | The Lemoine Company |
| Landscape Architect | Jon Emerson & Associates |
| Structural Engineer | McKee & Deville Consulting Engineers, Inc. |
| MEP Engineer | M & E Consultants |
| Civil Engineer | C.H. Fenstermaker Associates |
| Lighting Design | PHA Lighting Design |
| Museum Programming | M. Goodwin Associates, Inc. |
| Fountain Design | Fluidity Design Consultants, Inc. |
| Photographers | Timothy Hursley |
| | Philip Gould (pg. 174-175, 187) |

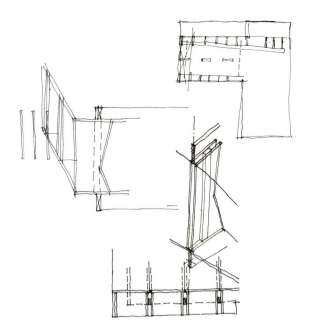

# PROSPECT.1 WELCOME CENTER
NEW ORLEANS, LOUISIANA

Prospect.1 New Orleans [P.1], the largest biennial of international contemporary art ever organized in the United States, exhibited 81 artists in museums, historic buildings and found sites throughout the city of New Orleans. The Welcome Center structure created for this art biennial was housed in one of these found spaces — an empty historic warehouse in downtown New Orleans — with the intent to orient visitors to the city and the biennial.

To accomplish this goal, a 400-square-foot structure was initially inspired by the shape and scale of shipping containers, a nod to the significance of the port to the city's economy and a reference to the nature of delivery for much of the art exhibited for the biennial. Due to constraints of time and budget (the entire project was designed pro bono and constructed in less than six weeks at a total cost of $28,000), a single construction material was selected that was both inexpensive and readily available. Utilizing construction-grade plywood as floor, wall, ceiling and structure, the form of the Welcome Center is manipulated to

provide a hospitality desk, display counter, refreshment center and seating bench for visitors. Acting as a container within a container, the ribbed plywood exterior construction acts in dialogue with the wood structure of the historic warehouse, contrasting the architecture of old and new.

In an effort to maintain the "found" nature of the space, minimal modifications were made to the remainder of the warehouse to accommodate the new functions of art display and visitor orientation. Simple, utilitarian spot lights were provided as part of new electrical service to the building, new emergency exiting to accommodate life safety codes was added, and a new steel and polycarbonate entry door was installed to secure the space. This new door contrasts with the historic character of the warehouse and provides a glowing street presence at night to signal to visitors the unique nature of the container within.

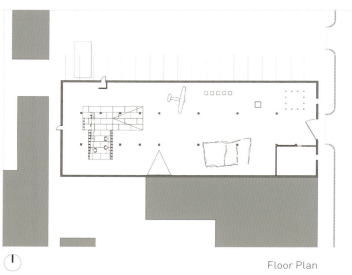

Floor Plan

The Welcome Center occupies the rear of an existing warehouse, drawing visitors past artworks that include "Dreamer" by Paul Villinski (right) and "Social Dress New Orleans — 730 Days After" by Takashi Horisaki (left).

In order to expedite construction of the Welcome Center, a digital model, along with a complete set of cut templates, was developed to clearly and accurately describe the design intent to the contractor.

A total of 115 sheets of construction-grade plywood were used, with the majority of the work milled and prefabricated off-site. With this approach, final on-site assembly of the structure was able to be completed in less than one week.

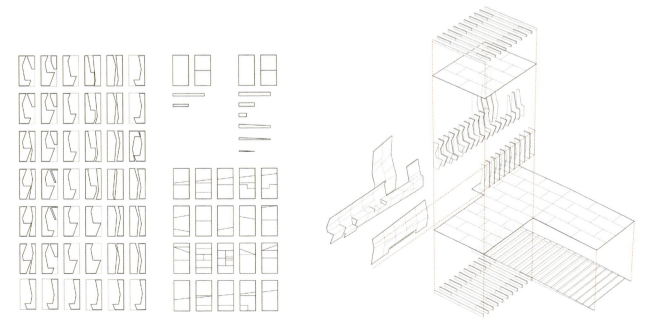

199

| | |
|---|---|
| Client | U.S. Biennial, Inc. |
| Architect of Record | Eskew+Dumez+Ripple |
| Project Team | Steve Dumez, Thaddeus Zarse, Nicole Marshall |
| General Contractor | Canal Construction of Louisiana, LLC |
| Furnishings | Associated Office Systems (AOS) |
| Photographers | Will Crocker |
| | Steve Dumez (pg. 192-193, 195, 197-198) |

# L.B. LANDRY HIGH SCHOOL
NEW ORLEANS, LOUISIANA

This post-Katrina replacement high school for the Louisiana Department of Education's Recovery School District was commissioned in the wake of Hurricane Katrina as one of the first high schools rebuilt after the storm. The original school was founded in 1938 as the first high school in Algiers that African-American residents could attend and only the second black high school established in Orleans Parish, therefore retaining a significant place in the city's history.

The design establishes academic "houses" for each high school grade level. These are provided within two featured classroom wings, located at the second and third floors of the building. Located below the classrooms are the school library and a neighborhood health clinic, each designed to allow independent access to the public for after-hours use. These wings are organized to create a central courtyard for use as an outdoor gathering space for the student body focused around a mature existing magnolia tree that was retained on the site. The courtyard is wrapped with expansive glazing connecting the interior spaces with the outdoors.

The public assembly spaces of the auditorium and gymnasium are located at the second floor, where an expansive public lobby is accessed by a monumental stair. Here, a graphic "ribbon" of inspirational quotes wraps the upper walls of the double-height space. Overhead, a large clerestory is strategically located above the perforated metal ceiling that washes the space with daylight that changes constantly over the course of the day.

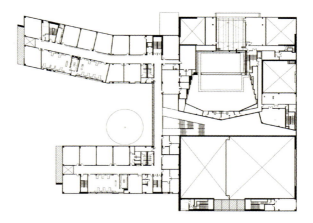

Third Floor Plan

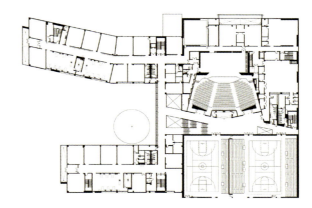

Second Floor Plan

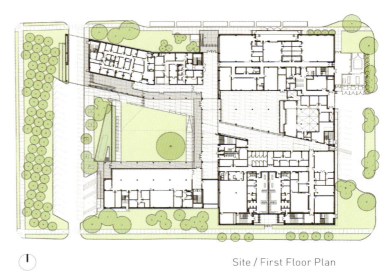

Site / First Floor Plan

The building incorporates numerous sustainable design strategies, with a LEED for Schools Silver certification anticipated. Many of these, including numerous daylighting strategies, solar controls, stormwater management system and photovoltaic energy harvesting system, were designed as highly visible, didactic elements of the project for use as teaching tools for faculty and students.

Due to the constraints of the relatively small urban site, public program elements typically located at grade such as the auditorium and two gymnasiums were elevated to the second floor, accessed by a large, monumental stair. This allows school-wide program elements to remain central in the building while also allowing for much-needed green space on the site.

| | |
|---|---|
| Client | Louisiana Department of Education, Recovery School District |
| Architect of Record | Eskew+Dumez+Ripple |
| Project Team | Steve Dumez, Tracy Lea, Randy Hutchison, Amanda Rivera, |
| | Cynthia Dubberley, Wendy Kerrigan, Jennifer Pelc, |
| | Robert Kleinpeter, Jason Richards, Dru Lamb, |
| | David Demsey, Thaddeus Zarse, Cecile Richards |
| Associate Architect | SHW Group LLP |
| General Contractor | Satterfield & Pontikes Construction Group, LLC |
| Landscape Architect | Daly Sublette Landscape Architects, Inc. |
| Structural Engineer | Schrenk & Peterson Consulting Engineers, Inc. |
| MEP Engineer | Moses Engineers |
| Civil Engineer | Schrenk & Peterson Consulting Engineers, Inc. |
| Geotechnical Engineer | Eustis Engineering Company |
| Food Service Consultant | Futch Design Associates |
| Acoustical/Audio-Visual | Gracenote Consulting |
| Sustainability Consultant | FutureProof |
| Photographer | Timothy Hursley |

**APPENDIX**

# ACKNOWLEDGEMENTS

R. ALLEN ESKEW, FAIA

In the spring of 1986, four young architects, united in the excitement of a new vision for a "modernist" architectural practice based in New Orleans, established the firm of Eskew, Vogt, Salvato & Filson.

Lloyd Vogt and I had been considering an architectural life together since our undergraduate days at Louisiana State University, in Baton Rouge. Leonard Salvato arrived in New Orleans from New York in 1982 with an invitation from our mentor, Charles Moore, to join the 1984 World Fair design studio in the architectural offices of Perez Associates. Ron Filson, having discovered the charms of New Orleans when working with Charles Moore, Malcolm Heard and myself on the 1974 Piazza d'Italia competition, moved to the Crescent City from Los Angeles in 1979 to become the Dean of Architecture at Tulane University. As a young group, we four made for a good mix of talent, experience and scholarship, all united by a youthful, entrepreneurial spirit.

By 1989, Salvato and Vogt had returned to individual practices as Ron and I established a new partnership, Eskew Filson Architects. In 1997, the practice was consolidated as Eskew+ and soon relocated to our current riverfront studio. The 2000 millennial milestone marked the next expansion of the studio's leadership team to include Steve Dumez, Mark Ripple, Chuck Hite and Tracy Lea. These four joined me as Directors and the firm was renamed Eskew+Dumez+Ripple. Most recently, in 2010, Kurt Hagstette and Jenifer Navard were named Directors and joined our leadership team. Together, we safely steered the firm through the trauma of Hurricane Katrina and the challenges of recovering our practice, our home, and our community. Such tempering under fire has strengthened both our partnership and our creativity.

We recognize that we live in a truly unique place with a valid claim to the authenticity of its food, music, architecture, landscape and social rituals. We see New Orleans as a vibrant architectural laboratory, complemented with an extraordinary inventory of historical precedents. Richly informative examples of how to make beautiful architecture and sustainable urban fabric abound in this place.

Today, Eskew+Dumez+Ripple thrives in the New Orleans landscape of recovery and reinvention, while also contributing our accumulated expertise to a number of communities around the region. We always endeavor to complement our core professional contributions of architecture and planning with our responsibilities for active civic participation and cultural arts engagement.

We gratefully acknowledge the depth of creative collaborators in our studio over the years, and their talents can be seen in the buildings and places we have created. We include them herein by year of participation so that their tenures might mark and cross-reference the ebb and flows of growing an architectural practice.

The creation of this monograph could not have have been successfully completed without the passion and persistence of Nicole Marshall and Magen Gladden. Nicole was the ever-present coordinator of content and substance while Magen consistently finessed the graphic design framework. Clearly evidenced in the photographic documentation in this book is the magic of Tim Hursley, the long-standing chronicler of our body of work. The clarity of Tim's photographic eye consistently frames the personality of our projects.

Their work, under the constant leadership of Steve Dumez, along with Gordon Goff at ORO Editions, has allowed us to capture the spirit of our creative community at Eskew+Dumez+Ripple. And most importantly, we honor our family and friends who have stood by us all as we have stayed this course and savored the creative adventure.

z Visitor Center

arolina Aquarium

n M. Shaw
eral Courthouse

Estuarine Habitats & Coastal
Fisheries Research Center

Shell River Road Museum

New Orleans
Fairgrounds Racetrack

Community of Joy Church

International Game Fish
Association Hall of Fame
and Museum

Ochsner Clinic Foundation
Medical Library

Riverwalk Marketplace

White Linen Bathing Pavilion

Pine Jog Environmental
Education Center

Capitol Park Interpretive Plan

Red Sea Aquarium In Jeddah

Lasalle State Office Building

Audubon Institute
Strategic Plan

Keating Magee
Advertising Offices

St. Peter Parish Church
Multi-Purpose Facility

W Hotel New Orleans

W Hotel French Quarter

## 1994

n Anderson
hris Brooks
er Doncaster
ynn Drury
eve Dumez
ck Dupont
llen Eskew
Ron Filson
irginia Fox
ris Harris
huck Hite
ry Hoffman
ncy Kaiser
Kleinpeter
Tracy Lea
ck Marshall
eslie Myers
nise Peytral
ark Ripple
aki Smith
ndi Stroud
iam Vincent
hn Wallace

## 1995

John Anderson
Loren Berot
Chris Brooks
Steven Dangermond
Mary Ditcharo
Peter Doncaster
Lynn Drury
Steve Dumez
Rick Dupont
Allen Eskew
Ron Filson
Virginia Fox
Greg Gardiol
Iris Harris
Chuck Hite
Gary Hoffman
Bob Kleinpeter
Douglas Kocher
Tracy Lea
Amanda Lehmann
Nick Marshall
Jennifer Martinez
Diane Mouton
Leslie Myers
William Peterson
Denise Peytral
Ronald Pilgrim
Mark Ripple
B J Seigel
Kaki Smith
Gabe Smith
Sandi Stroud
William Vincent
John Wallace
Debra Warner

## 1996

John Anderson
Loren Berot
Chris Brooks
Jennifer Calla
Steven Dangermond
Mary Ditcharo
Peter Doncaster
Steve Dumez
Rick Dupont
Allen Eskew
Ron Filson
Virginia Fox
Greg Gardiol
Iris Harris
Chuck Hite
Gary Hoffman
Bob Kleinpeter
Tracy Lea
Nick Marshall
Jennifer Martinez
Diane Mouton
Leslie Myers
Denise Peytral
Mark Ripple
B J Seigel
Gabe Smith
John Wallace
Brien Watson
Debra Warner

## 1997

Jose Alvarez
John Anderson
Eric Becker
Jennifer Calla
Steve Dumez
Rick Dupont
Allen Eskew
Virginia Fox
Iris Harris
Chuck Hite
Gary Hoffman
Bob Kleinpeter
Lisa Lamont
Tracy Lea
Marianne Makdisi
Nick Marshall
Diane Mouton
Denise Peytral
Mark Ripple
Ashley Schafer
B J Seigel
Gabe Smith
Brett Spearman
John Wallace
Debra Warner

## 1998

Jose Alvarez
John Anderson
Eric Becker
Jennifer Calla
Steve Dumez
Rick Dupont
Allen Eskew
Virginia Fox
Denise France
Beth Fulmer
Iris Harris
Chuck Hite
Gary Hoffman
Bob Kleinpeter
Lisa Lamont
Tracy Lea
Nick Marshall
Alan McGillivray
Diane Mouton
Mark Ripple
B J Seigel
Gabe Smith

## 1999

Milady Almanzar
Jose Alvarez
John Anderson
Vince Bandy
Julie Charvat
Steve Dumez
Rick Dupont
Allen Eskew
Virginia Fox
Eric Giardina
Iris Harris
Chuck Hite
Bob Kleinpeter
Matt Kymes
Lisa Lamont
Tracy Lea
Nick Marshall
Ellen McLean
Tyler Meyr
Kevin Morris
Byron Mouton
Diane Mouton
Mark Ripple
Timothy Schmidt
B J Seigel
Gabe Smith

Aquarium of the Americas
Phase I

Baton Rouge Riverfront
Master Plan

Jean Lafitte Environmental
Education Center

National Wetlands
Research Center

Underwater World
Mall Of America

New Orleans Museum Of Art

LSU Life Sciences
Building Annex

Aquarium of the Americas
Phase II

Estuarium: A Marine Science
& Interpretive Center

Audubon Center for the
Research of Endangered
Species

Natche

South C

Jo

U.S. Fe

## 1989

Mac Ball
Donald del Cid
Georgia Dufresne
Susanna Eisenman
Allen Eskew
Nancy Eskew
Ron Filson
Virginia Fox
Kristin Grainger
Chuck Hite
David Keiffer
Bob Kleinpeter
Jules Lagarde
John McDonald
Alan McGillvray
Mark Ripple
Steve Rome
Leonard Salvato
Kaki Smith
Charles Sterkx
Carol Trahan
Richard Veith
Luis Vildostegui
Lloyd Vogt
John Wettermark

## 1990

Georgia Dufresne
Susanna Eisenman
Allen Eskew
Nancy Eskew
Ron Filson
Chuck Hite
Gary Hoffman
David Keiffer
Bob Kleinpeter
Jules Lagarde
Byron Mouton
Adam Newman
Mark Ripple
Steve Rome
B J Seigel
Kaki Smith
Anita Songy
John Wettermark
Michelle Zande

## 1991

Georgia Dufresne
Susanna Eisenman
Allen Eskew
Ron Filson
Anne Glynn
Iris Harris
Chuck Hite
Gary Hoffman
Bob Kleinpeter
Jules Lagarde
Dori Levy
Byron Mouton
Denise Peytral
Mark Ripple
Steve Rome
B J Seigel
Kaki Smith
Michelle Zande

## 1992

Chris Brooks
Susanna Eisenman
Allen Eskew
Ron Filson
Anne Glynn
Iris Harris
Chuck Hite
Gary Hoffman
Bob Kleinpeter
Judy Lee
Denise Peytral
Linna Richardson
Mark Ripple
B J Seigel
Kaki Smith

## 1993

Chris Brooks
Allen Eskew
Ron Filson
Virginia Fox
Iris Harris
Chuck Hite
Gary Hoffman
Nancy Kaiser
Bob Kleinpeter
Tracy Lea
Nick Marshall
Tammy Mets
Denise Peytral
Mark Ripple
B J Seigel
Kaki Smith
Sandi Stroud

Jo
C
Pet
L
S
R
A

V

C
Ga
N
Bo

Ni
Le
De
M
K
Sa
Wil
Jo

**COLLABORATORS**

| | | | | |
|---|---|---|---|---|
| ...ked Creek | Apalachicola National Estuarine Research Coastal Education Center | 930 Poydras Residential Tower | Children's Hospital of New Orleans CICU/PICU | Samuel J. Green Charter School Edible Kitchen | LA/SPCA Animal Rescue & Care Center |

Children's Hospital
of New Orleans CICU/PICU

Samuel J. Green Charter
School Edible Kitchen

LA/SPCA Animal Rescue
& Care Center

Apalachicola National
Estuarine Research Coastal
Education Center

930 Poydras Residential Tower

New Orleans
BioInnovation Center

U.S. Mint Jazz Theatre

Champions Square

...servatory
Center

Cypress Bend Office Building

Trumpet Advertising
Headquarters

Reinventing the Crescent:
New Orleans Riverfront Plan

Prospect.1 Welcome Center

NOCCA Master Plan:
A 100-Year Vision

Veterans Affairs
Replacement Medical Center,
Pan Am Life Building

...er Plan

Bridge House Rehabilitative
Care Center

Gulf Coast Bank & Trust
Carrollton Branch

Louisiana Superdome
Enhancements

Ochsner North Campus
Expansion

...rena

University Of New Orleans
Master Plan

...ea House

Graham's Bayou Nature
Center

L.B. Landry High School

Lamar Advertising
Headquarters

Acadiana Center for the Arts
Phase II

Transfiguration of The Lord
Church

...ademy
...oration

Global Green USA Sustainable
Housing Design

Make It Right
Prototype House

Rosa F. Keller Library
& Community Center

Veterans Affairs Replacement
Medical Center

Tulane Library Expansion

## 2006

Jose Alvarez
John Anderson
Leslie Bergeron
Steve Dumez
Rick Dupont
Allen Eskew
Brett Gauthier
Kurt Hagstette
Stephanie Hart
Chuck Hite
David Hurd
Bob Kleinpeter
Lauren Lacey
Tracy Lea
Alan Lewis
Carol Mockbee
Jenifer Navard
Jenny Pelc
Cecile Richards
Mark Ripple
Amanda Rivera
Joy Robinson
Jack Sawyer
David Smith
Jessica Stumpf
Carl Westerman
Sky Williams

## 2007

Jose Alvarez
John Anderson
Leslie Bergeron
David Demsey
Cynthia Dubberley
Jay Dufour
Steve Dumez
Rick Dupont
Allen Eskew
Brett Gauthier
Kurt Hagstette
Chuck Hite
Tom Holloman
Randy Hutchison
Wendy Kerrigan
Bob Kleinpeter
Lauren Lacey
Dru Lamb
Tracy Lea
Alan Lewis
Nicole Marshall
Carol Mockbee
Jenifer Navard
Jenny Pelc
Shawn Preau
Cecile Richards
Jason Richards
Mark Ripple
Amanda Rivera
Joy Robinson
Jack Sawyer
Paul Sieberth
Rainier Simoneaux
David Smith
Jessica Stumpf
Sky Williams
Thaddeus Zarse

## 2008

Jose Alvarez
Leslie Bergeron
Randy D'Amico
David Demsey
Cynthia Dubberley
Jay Dufour
Steve Dumez
Rick Dupont
Allen Eskew
Kurt Hagstette
Chuck Hite
Randy Hutchison
Wendy Kerrigan
Bob Kleinpeter
Lauren Lacey
Dru Lamb
Tracy Lea
Nicole Magnelia
Nicole Marshall
Marty McElveen
Jenifer Navard
Jenny Pelc
Aaron Pexa
Kristen Preau
Shawn Préau
Cecile Richards
Jason Richards
Mark Ripple
Amanda Rivera
Jack Sawyer
Paul Sieberth
Jessica Stumpf
Sky Williams
Thaddeus Zarse

## 2009

Leslie Bergeron
Randy D'Amico
David Demsey
Cynthia Dubberley
Steve Dumez
Rick Dupont
Allen Eskew
Magen Raine Gladden
Kurt Hagstette
Chuck Hite
Randy Hutchison
Michael Keller
Wendy Kerrigan
Bob Kleinpeter
Lauren Lacey
Dru Lamb
Tracy Lea
Nicole Marshall
Adam Martin
Marty McElveen
Jenifer Navard
Lynn Ostenson
Jenny Pelc
Aaron Pexa
Shawn Préau
Jason Richards
Mark Ripple
Amanda Rivera
Jack Sawyer
Paul Sieberth
Z Smith
Jessica Stumpf
Kim Tseng
Jennie West
Isaac Williams
Sky Williams

## 2010

Jose Alvarez
Leslie Bergeron
David Demsey
Aseem Deshpande
Cynthia Dubberley
Tim Dumatrait
Steve Dumez
Rick Dupont
Allen Eskew
Magen Raine Gladden
Kurt Hagstette
Chuck Hite
Randy Hutchison
Michael Keller
Wendy Kerrigan
Bob Kleinpeter
Matthew Kymes
Lauren Lacey
Dru Lamb
Tracy Lea
Nicole Marshall
Adam Martin
Shelley Maxwell
Marty McElveen
Scott Melançon
Jenifer Navard
Lynn Ostenson
Jenny Pelc
Aaron Pexa
Shawn Préau
Jason Richards
Mark Ripple
Amanda Rivera
Christian Rodriguez
Jack Sawyer
Jay Seastrunk
Paul Sieberth
Z Smith
Jessica Stumpf
Kim Tseng
Jennie West
Isaac Williams
Sky Williams

Louisiana State Museum

Kate And Laurance
Eustis Chapel

Lieselotte Tansey
Breast Center
at Ochsner Clinic

Downtown Development
District Office

Children's Hospital
of New Orleans
Emergency Department/
Operating Room

New Orleans Metropolitan
Convention and Visitors'
Bureau Headquarters

Bienville State Office Building

Baton Rouge
Riverfront Master Plan

St. Martha Catholic Church

Santa Barbara
Museum Of Natural History

Shaw Center For The Arts

River Bend Environmental
Education Center

Beaufort NCNERR/NOAA
Laboratory

Whitney National Bank
Carrollton Branch

Paul and Lulu Hilliard
Univeristy Art Museum

Acadiana Center for the Arts

Ochsner Medical Center
for Children

University Of Louisiana
Monroe College
of Health Sciences

Desoto Riverfront Park
Concept Plan

Copper District
Urban Design Study

Dr. Nancy Foster Florida Keys
Environmental Center

Bozeman Fish Technology
Center

Xavier University Master Plan

Mississippi River Road
Interpretive Plan

Chattanooga Outdoor Center

Neonatal Intensive Care Unit
Children's Hospital
of New Orleans

Louisiana Immersive
Technologies Enterprise

Rivercamps at Croc

LIGO Livingston O
Science Education

Riversphere Mas

New Orleans A
Restoratio

Southern Living Id

Mount Carmel A
High School Res

## 2000

Milady Almanzar
Jose Alvarez
John Anderson
Vince Bandy
Julie Charvat
Wen Chen
Shannon Downey
Kathlyn Driscoll-Lopez
Steve Dumez
Rick Dupont
Allen Eskew
Virginia Fox
Kurt Hagstette
Iris Harris
Chuck Hite
Bob Kleinpeter
Matt Kymes
Tracy Lea
Nick Marshall
Ellen McLean
Kevin Morris
Byron Mouton
Diane Mouton
Hector Palacios
Mark Ripple
Stacey Schexnayder
Gabe Smith
Vicki Smith
Kevin Spurgeon

## 2001

Milady Almanzar
Jose Alvarez
John Anderson
Vince Bandy
Julie Charvat
Wen Chen
Shannon Downey
Kathlyn Driscoll-Lopez
Steve Dumez
Rick Dupont
Allen Eskew
Virginia Fox
Kurt Hagstette
Iris Harris
Chuck Hite
Bob Kleinpeter
Matt Kymes
Jodi Laumer-Giddens
Tracy Lea
Nick Marshall
Kevin Morris
Byron Mouton
Diane Mouton
Hector Palacios
Mark Ripple
Sebastian Salvado
Gabe Smith
Vicki Smith

## 2002

Jose Alvarez
John Anderson
Vince Bandy
Julie Charvat
Rami Diaz
Shannon Downey
Steve Dumez
Rick Dupont
Allen Eskew
Virginia Fox
Kurt Hagstette
Jacqueline Handy
Iris Harris
Chuck Hite
Bob Kleinpeter
Tracy Lea
Alan Lewis
Nick Marshall
Kevin Moore
Kevin Morris
Byron Mouton
Diane Mouton
Hector Palacios
Mark Ripple
Sebastian Salvado
Gabe Smith
Vicki Smith
Kiyomi Troemner
Carl Westerman

## 2003

Jose Alvarez
John Anderson
Vince Bandy
Leslie Bergeron
Julie Charvat
Katy Clausen
Rami Diaz
Shannon Downey
Steve Dumez
Rick Dupont
Blaise Durio
Allen Eskew
Virginia Fox
Kurt Hagstette
Jacqueline Handy
Iris Harris
Chuck Hite
Bob Kleinpeter
Tracy Lea
Alan Lewis
Nick Marshall
Lisa McConnell
Kevin Moore
Kevin Morris
Byron Mouton
Diane Mouton
Jenifer Navard
Hector Palacios
Mark Ripple
Amanda Rivera
Joy Robinson
Sebastian Salvado
Katherine Sauter
Jay Seastrunk
Catharine Smith
Gabe Smith
Vicki Smith
Kiyomi Troemner
Carl Westerman

## 2004

Jose Alvarez
John Anderson
Leslie Bergeron
Rami Diaz
Shannon Downey
Steve Dumez
Rick Dupont
Blaise Durio
Allen Eskew
Virginia Fox
Kurt Hagstette
Trena Hill
Chuck Hite
Bob Kleinpeter
Tracy Lea
Alan Lewis
Kyle Libersat
Nick Marshall
Kevin Moore
Kevin Morris
Jenifer Navard
Hector Palacios
Mark Ripple
Amanda Rivera
Joy Robinson
Sebastian Salvado
Katherine Sauter
Jay Seastrunk
Katy Clausen
Gabe Smith
Vicki Smith
Kiyomi Troemner
Carl Westerman

## 2005

Jose Alvare
John Anders
Leslie Berge
David Desho
Rami Diaz
Shannon Dow
Steve Dume
Rick Dupor
Blaise Duri
Allen Eske
Virginia Fo
Kurt Hagste
Trena Hill
Chuck Hit
David Hur
Bob Kleinpe
Tracy Lea
Alan Lewis
Nick Marsh
Kevin Moo
Kevin Morr
Jenifer Nava
Hector Palac
Jenny Pel
Mark Ripp
Amanda Riv
Joy Robinso
Katherine Sa
Jack Sawye
Jay Seastru
Gabe Smit
Vicki Smit
Kiyomi Troem
Carl Western

# CONTRIBUTOR BIOGRAPHIES

**William Morrish**

William Rees Morrish is Dean of the School of Constructed Environments, and Associate Dean for Parsons The New School of Design in New York City. He is a nationally recognized urban designer and architect whose practice encompasses inter-disciplinary research on urban housing and infrastructure, collaborative publications on human settlement and community design, and educational programs exploring integrated design, which are applied to a wide range of innovative, community-based city projects.

Drawing from the disciplines of architecture, landscape architecture, planning and architectural history, his work engages citizens and civic leaders in the act of giving visual representation and form to the complex infrastructural, cultural and ecological systems that link residents to community, city to region, and local to global. Identifying points of convergence between systems, he defines principles making the connections between nature to humans, and humans to humans, tangible. From these places, he constructs sustainable urban spaces and practices based on the everyday economic and ecological transactions of the local urban society. He is the author/co-author of several books including *Civilizing Terrains*, and co-authored *Building for the Arts, Planning To Stay and Growing Urban Habitats*.

**Reed Kroloff**

Reed Kroloff is the Director of the Cranbrook Academy of Art and Museum in Bloomfield Hills, Michigan, and an independent architectural consultant and commentator.

Mr. Kroloff previously served as the Editor-in-Chief of *Architecture* magazine. Under his direction, *Architecture* received distinguished awards for editorial and design excellence, and quickly became the leading design publication in the nation. His writing has appeared in many other magazines and newspapers as well, ranging from *Metropolis* to *Artforum*, and he has been profiled by publications such as the *New York Times*.

Mr. Kroloff writes and lectures widely, and is a regular visiting critic at architecture schools and professional organizations across the country. He holds degrees from the University of Texas at Austin and Yale University, and has practiced architecture in Texas and Arizona. Mr. Kroloff serves on numerous boards and advisory councils, ranging from the Register of Peer Professionals of the United States General Services Administration to the Public Architecture Foundation. Mr. Kroloff served as Dean of the Tulane University School of Architecture, 2004-07.

**Alex Krieger, FAIA**

Alex Krieger has combined a career of teaching and practice, dedicating himself in both to understanding how to improve the quality of place and life in our major urban areas. Mr. Krieger is founding principal of Chan Krieger NBBJ, the Cambridge, Massachusetts-based architecture and urban design studio of NBBJ, a global architecture firm. Offering services in architecture, urban design and planning since 1984, the studio has served a broad array of clients in over 30 cities, focusing primarily on educational, institutional, healthcare and public projects in complex urban settings.

Mr. Krieger is a professor at the Harvard Graduate School of Design, where he has taught since 1977. He recently served as Chairman of the Department of Urban Planning and Design from 1998-2004. He has authored several publications on urban design such as *Remaking the Urban Waterfront*, *Towns and Town Planning Principles* and *Past Futures: Two Centuries of Imagining Boston*. He has also authored more than two dozen essays on American urbanization for various publications and lectures frequently at national conferences and universities.

**Lawrence Scarpa, FAIA**

The design work of Lawrence Scarpa has redefined the role of the architect to produce some of the most remarkable and exploratory work today. For Larry, each project appears as an opportunity to rethink the way things normally get done — with material, form, construction, even financing — and to subsequently redefine it to cull out its latent potentials (as Scarpa aptly describes: making the "ordinary extraordinary"). It is always deeply rooted in conditions of the everyday, and works with our perception and preconceptions to allow us to see things in new ways.

Over the last 10 years, Mr. Scarpa's architectural practice PUGH + SCARPA (recently rebranded BROOKS + SCARPA) has received more than 50 major design awards, notably 16 National AIA Awards, including the 2010 Architecture Firm Award from the American Institute of Architects, the 2006 and 2003 AIA Committee on the Environment "Top Ten Green Project" awards, among many others. He is also a co-founder of Livable Places, Inc., a Santa Monica, CA-based nonprofit development and public policy organization dedicated to building mixed-use housing on underutilized and problematic parcels of land.

## DIRECTOR BIOGRAPHIES

**R. Allen Eskew, FAIA**

Throughout his career, Allen Eskew has actively pursued architectural and planning projects that impact the public realm. Collaboration with colleagues and allied professionals has remained a central element to his design process. After receiving a Master of Architecture degree from the University of California, Berkeley following a Bachelor of Architecture degree from Louisiana State University, he relocated to New Orleans and soon became the Project Director for the 1984 Louisiana World Exposition.

Since founding his own design studio, Allen has spent much of his time involved in major civic developments throughout the country. Waterfront redevelopment initiatives, environmental education centers and cultural institutions have been a core focus of his professional engagement. Allen has also been heavily involved with a number of the urban planning efforts in the City of New Orleans, including the Unified New Orleans Plan (UNOP) following Hurricane Katrina, as well as "Reinventing the Crescent," a 6-mile Riverfront Development Plan. He was elected to the American Institute of Architects College of Fellows in 2003 and serves the local community through civic organizations such as the Council for a Better Louisiana, Unity for the Homeless and as a long-standing Board Member for the Contemporary Arts Center.

**Steve Dumez, FAIA**

Born and raised in South Louisiana, Steve Dumez received his Bachelor of Architecture from Louisiana State University in 1982. Following graduation, he moved to New Orleans to work with Allen Eskew on the 1984 Louisiana World Exposition, where he initiated a professional relationship that continues to this day. After departing the city for graduate study at Yale University, where he received a Master of Architecture degree, and following a period teaching and working in Los Angeles, Steve returned to New Orleans in 1994.

As Design Director for the firm, Steve has led the design efforts for the studio's numerous award-winning and nationally recognized projects. His role — as design critic, mentor and team leader on various projects — has contributed to the growth of numerous designers that have collaborated within the studio's practice. He has also served as president of the state and local chapters of the American Institute of Architects, and in 2007 was elected to the AIA College of Fellows.

**Mark Ripple, AIA, LEED AP**

Mark Ripple has centered his entire professional career in New Orleans since graduation from Louisiana State University in 1979. After joining Allen Eskew in 1989, Mark served as project architect for a wide range of civic and institutional projects prior to his designation as Director in 2000. While focused on market sector responsibilities in healthcare, laboratories and environmental projects, Mark also serves as the internal studio operations leader.

The son of a residential contractor, Mark brings a balance of pragmatism and constructability to the design process, with particular interest in technically and programmatically challenging assignments. His commitment to collaborative problem solving with clients and colleagues has inspired several long-term client relationships, including Children's Hospital of New Orleans, the Archdiocese of New Orleans and the Ochsner Clinic Foundation. Committed to the causes of several local nonprofits and community initiatives, Mark continues to contribute to the rebirth of the city he loves as a resource wherever he can.

### Tracy Lea, AIA, LEED AP BD+C

Tracy Lea has enjoyed a fulfilling professional career built around translating concepts into reality. Focusing in the realm of emerging technology, environmental sustainability and integrated design, Tracy has combined design sensitivity with an expertise in construction technology into a practical project approach. In 1993, he relocated to New Orleans following 15 years of professional practice in San Francisco, and joined the practice of Eskew+Dumez+Ripple.

In addition to project responsibilities, Tracy oversees the firm's Information Technology systems and is the in-house resource for zoning and code compliance, universal barrier-free design and green building practices. He is an NCARB-registered architect and holds a Bachelor of Architecture and B.S. in Environmental Design from Auburn University. He is also actively involved in the American Institute of Architects, has served several terms on the AIA-Louisiana Executive Board and is a professional member of the International Code Council and the U.S. Green Building Council.

### Jenifer Navard

As a native of New Orleans and a graduate of the University of Louisiana at Lafayette, Jenifer Navard has kept her roots in Louisiana, practicing at multiple scales of business management for the last 25 years. As a Certified Public Accountant, her professional experience ranges from auditing with one of the nations top five public accounting firms, through financial accounting for SEC firms and the management of mid-sized companies in a diverse range of industries. Since joining Eskew+Dumez+Ripple in 2003, Jenifer has served as the studio's Chief Financial Officer.

She works closely with all firm Directors and Project Managers to ensure adherence to both the design and business values within each project that we undertake and spends much time training architectural staff on necessary project management skills. Jenifer is a passionate advocate for the free reign of creativity in the studio and works tirelessly to help that take place within a successful, productive business model. Additionally, she manages all other non-architectural matters of the studio and oversees the firm's strategic planning efforts.

### Charles Hite, AIA, CSI

A native of Lewiston, New York, Chuck attended Louisiana State University, where he received his Bachelor of Architecture in 1976. Having become a "Southerner" in this short time at LSU, he chose to make his home in New Orleans, where he has since practiced throughout his professional life. In 1982 his career path intersected with Allen Eskew (at Perez Associates) and he began a working relationship that originated with the 1984 Louisiana World Exposition.

As a team collaborator, Chuck provided key design and project management leadership on the New Orleans Museum of Art, South Carolina Aquarium, National Wetlands Research Center, Estuarine Habitats & Fisheries Center and the Paul and Lulu Hilliard Art Museum in Lafayette. His design and technical engineering background has made him a valuable resource and mentor to the many young design professionals throughout the firm. In addition to his project responsibilities Chuck manages the firm's Contract Administration processes and assists in project staffing.

### Kurt Hagstette, AIA

Kurt Hagstette has turned his youthful appreciation of construction and design into a successful career in architecture. After graduating from Louisiana State University with a Bachelor of Architecture degree in 1978, his career focused on the design and production of complex civic cultural and sports entertainment projects in southern Louisiana. Most notable of these are Lafayette's Acadiana Center for the Arts and the New Orleans Arena. After working for a number of years with New Orleans' famed Arthur Q. Davis, Kurt joined Eskew+Dumez+Ripple in 2000.

In his management position with the firm, he consistently applies years of experience and knowledge in building construction and detailing to all facets of projects under his leadership, while maintaining a keen interest in emerging building technologies. A proactive Project Manager and mentor, Kurt works closely with emerging professionals in the studio to educate them in strong project management practices and client communications techniques. As a native of New Orleans, Kurt has also provided key leadership in the recovery of the City's Broadmoor neighborhood in the years since Hurricane Katrina.

ORO editions
Publishers of Architecture, Art, and Design
Gordon Goff: Publisher

USA, ASIA, EUROPE, MIDDLE EAST
www.oroeditions.com
info@oroeditions.com

Copyright © 2011 by ORO editions
ISBN: 978-0-9826226-2-9

Graphic Design: Magen Raine Gladden / Eskew+Dumez+Ripple,
Usana Shadday / OROeditions
Production Assistance: Gabriel Ely / OROeditions
Project Coordinator: Christy LaFaver / OROeditions
Edited by: Nicole Marshall / Eskew+Dumez+Ripple
Text: Steve Dumez, Nicole Marshall

Color Separations and Printing: ORO Group Ltd.
Printed in China.

Text printed using offset sheetfed printing process in 5 color on 157gsm premium matt
art paper with an off-line gloss acqueous spot varnish applied to all photographs.

ORO editions has made every effort to minimize the overall carbon footprint of this
project. As part of this goal, ORO editions, in association with Global ReLeaf, have
arranged to plant two trees for each and every tree used in the manufacturing of
the paper produced for this book. Global ReLeaf is an international campaign run by
American Forests, the nation's oldest nonprofit conservation organization. Global ReLeaf
is American Forests' education and action program that helps individuals, organizations,
agencies, and corporations improve the local and global environment by planting and
caring for trees.

North American Distribution:
Publishers Group West / Perseus
1700 Fourth Street
Berkeley, CA 94710, USA
www.pgw.com

International Distribution:
www.oroeditions.com